Measuring What Matters Most

This report was made possible by grants from the John D. and Catherine T. MacArthur Foundation in connection with its grant making initiative on Digital Media and Learning. For more information on the initiative visit http://www.macfound.org.

The John D. and Catherine T. MacArthur Foundation Reports on Digital Media and Learning

Peer Participation and Software: What Mozilla Has to Teach Government, by David R. Booth

The Future of Learning Institutions in a Digital Age, by Cathy N. Davidson and David Theo Goldberg with the assistance of Zoë Marie Jones

The Future of Thinking: Learning Institutions in a Digital Age, by Cathy N. Davidson and David Theo Goldberg with the assistance of Zoë Marie Jones

Kids and Credibility: An Empirical Examination of Youth, Digital Media Use, and Information Credibility, by Andrew J. Flanagin and Miriam Metzger with Ethan Hartsell, Alex Markov, Ryan Medders, Rebekah Pure, and Elisia Choi

New Digital Media and Learning as an Emerging Area and "Worked Examples" as One Way Forward, by James Paul Gee

Digital Media and Technology in Afterschool Programs, Libraries, and Museums, by Becky Herr-Stephenson, Diana Rhoten, Dan Perkel, and Christo Sims with contributions from Anne Balsamo, Maura Klosterman, and Susana Smith Bautista

Living and Learning with New Media: Summary of Findings from the Digital Youth Project, by Mizuko Ito, Heather Horst, Matteo Bittanti, danah boyd, Becky Herr-Stephenson, Patricia G. Lange, C. J. Pascoe, and Laura Robinson with Sonja Baumer, Rachel Cody, Dilan Mahendran, Katynka Z. Martínez, Dan Perkel, Christo Sims, and Lisa Tripp

Young People, Ethics, and the New Digital Media: A Synthesis from the GoodPlay Project, by Carrie James with Katie Davis, Andrea Flores, John M. Francis, Lindsay Pettingill, Margaret Rundle, and Howard Gardner

Confronting the Challenges of Participatory Culture: Media Education for the 21st Century, by Henry Jenkins (PI) with Ravi Purushotma, Margaret Weigel, Katie Clinton, and Alice J. Robison

The Civic Potential of Video Games, by Joseph Kahne, Ellen Middaugh, and Chris Evans

Quest to Learn: Developing the School for Digital Kids, by Katie Salen, Robert Torres, Loretta Wolozin, Rebecca Rufo-Tepper, and Arana Shapiro

Measuring What Matters Most: Choice-Based Assessments for the Digital Age, by Daniel L. Schwartz and Dylan Arena

Learning at Not-School? A Review of Study, Theory, and Advocacy for Education in Non-Formal Settings, by Julian Sefton-Green

Measuring What Matters Most

Choice-Based Assessments for the Digital Age

Daniel L. Schwartz and Dylan Arena

The MIT Press
Cambridge, Massachusetts
London, England

MIT Press books may be purchased at special quantity discounts for business or sales promotional use. For information, please email special_sales@mitpress.mit.edu or write to Special Sales Department, The MIT Press, 55 Hayward Street, Cambridge, MA 02142.

This book was set in Stone Serif and Stone Sans by the MIT Press. Printed and bound in the United States of America.

Library of Congress Cataloging-in-Publication Data

Schwartz, Daniel L.
Measuring what matters most : choice-based assessments for the digital age / Daniel L. Schwartz and Dylan Arena.
p. cm. — (The John D. and Catherine T. MacArthur Foundation reports on digital media and learning)
Includes bibliographical references.
ISBN 978-0-262-51837-6 (pbk. : alk. paper)
1. Educational tests and measurements—Data processing. 2. Decision-making—Evaluation. I. Arena, Dylan. II. Title.
LB3060.55.S39 2013
371.260285—dc23
2012029445

10 9 8 7 6 5 4 3 2 1

Contents

Series Foreword

The John D. and Catherine T. MacArthur Foundation Reports on Digital Media and Learning, published by the MIT Press in collaboration with the Monterey Institute for Technology and Education (MITE), present findings from current research on how young people learn, play, socialize, and participate in civic life. The reports result from research projects funded by the MacArthur Foundation as part of its fifty million dollar initiative in digital media and learning. They are published openly online (as well as in print) to support broad dissemination and stimulate further research in the field.

Acknowledgments

We would like to thank the members of the AAA Lab at Stanford University (http://aaalab.stanford.edu) for their contributions to the ideas and research presented here. Additionally, we wish to acknowledge their infinite patience when listening to the authors endlessly trying out pithy sentences in meetings. The development of this book and its ideas was supported by a grant from the MacArthur Foundation to James Gee, and then to the first author. The material includes work supported by the National Science Foundation under Grant No 0904324. Any opinions, findings, conclusions, or recommendations are those of the authors and do not necessarily reflect the views of the granting agencies.

I What Matters

1 Beliefs about Useful Learning

Educational assessment is a normative endeavor. The ideal assessment both reflects and reinforces educational goals that society deems valuable. One fundamental goal of education is to prepare students to act independently in the world—which is to say, make good choices. It follows that an ideal assessment would measure how well we are preparing students to do so. The argument of this report is that current assessments, which primarily focus on how much knowledge and skills students have accrued, are inadequate. Choice, rather than knowledge, should be the interpretative frame within which learning assessments are organized. Digital technologies make this possible, because interactive assessments can evaluate students in a context of choosing whether, what, how, and when to learn.

In education, most people see choice as a catalyst for learning. For instance, giving students choices can increase their motivation and learning (Iyengar and Lepper 1999). Choice is also important for learning, if only because students need to experience choices in the protected atmosphere of education so they can learn how to handle them before becoming independent.

The current assertion starts differently. It examines why choice should be viewed as the outcome of learning and not solely an instructional ingredient to improve learning. We contend that choice should be the interpretative framework for understanding learning outcomes. To achieve this reorientation in how people think about learning, assessment provides a powerful lever. Assessments shape the public mind, and everything else flows from that.

Assessment is not a sexy topic. It is tolerated as a necessary nuisance. This is the dulling fog that comes from accepting the premise that what exists must exist. Do not underestimate the power of assessments or the degree to which they have shaped how you think about learning.

Formulated in 1956, Benjamin Bloom's taxonomy of educational outcomes is still arguably one of the most influential frameworks for the design of instruction. It describes a pyramid of the following order, going from bottom to top: memory (called "knowledge" back then), comprehension, application, analysis, synthesis, and evaluation. Bloom's taxonomy was designed by a committee as an *assessment* framework, not an instructional one. It is not based on learning or pedagogical theory. Yet in the way that assessments always manage to do, it has commanded the instructional enterprise. Based on the pyramid, many people believe that students must first learn from the bottom of the pyramid (memorize) before engaging in higher-order thinking near the top (evaluate). This belief is wrong. Most people would recognize this if they could reclaim their common sense from the grip of assessment. For example, comprehension improves the formation of memories (Bransford and Johnson 1972), so making memories a prerequisite for comprehension does not work well. Similarly, having students learn a new topic in an application context is a great way to help them simultaneously learn the facts and evaluate their applications.

People have beliefs about learning that are mistaken. Current classroom and high-stakes assessments are largely responsible for this situation, because they send the wrong message about what matters. Teachers may tell students about the importance of persistence, critical thinking, interest development, and a host of other keys to a successful life. But tests provide the empirical evidence that students use to decide what is truly valued. If an assessment focuses on the retrieval and procedural application of narrow skills and facts, this is what students will think counts as useful learning. How can they not? It is the basis for promotion and approbation. By changing assessments to concentrate on choices, we should be able to improve beliefs about what constitutes useful learning.

There is a befuddling but extremely strong correlation in the Trends in International Mathematics and Science Study—an assessment taken by students around the world (http://timssandpirls.bc.edu). It is meant to help nations decide their standing. The study's actionable information is at the level of national policy rather than teachers and students. The odd finding is that the students of the nations that do the best on the test also exhibit the least "liking" of mathematics and science (e.g., Shen 2002). The better a nation scores on the math or science tests, the less interest the children there have in pursuing math or science. Nobody knows exactly why the negative correlation is so strong. There may be some statistical oddity that involves averaging individuals to compare nations (Robinson 1950). There are also more substantive possibilities. One is that students who do the best on these tests spend a lot of time learning with testlike questions. They interpret these questions as markers of what it means to have learned in science and mathematics. They do not like the vision that from their test-based vantage, learning is primarily an act of replicating what they have been told. It makes sense that they would not like math and science, despite doing well. They have missed the generative and contributive aspects of learning. Under this interpretation, rather than helping to prepare students for future learning in science and math, current assessments are propelling students to choose not to learn these domains.

Distortions of what counts as useful learning suffuse US culture. Our greatest fear is that those fortunate enough to have the resources to guide education may also have distorted visions of learning. What could be worse than creating educational technologies that become increasingly efficient at teaching the wrong thing? Successful people have gained many implicit lessons about what it took for them to achieve their successes, often accompanied by narratives of passion and perseverance. Yet these same people are at risk of supporting learning environments that ignore those lessons, and instead teach to outcomes that seem mostly important for standardized and end-of-chapter tests. Such is the sway of assessments.

The aim of assessment should be to advance the goals of society rather than misrepresent them. With new developments in technology, it should be possible to advance goals that were beyond the reach of prior assessments. To date, this has not been the case. Howard Wainer (2010, 17) argues that "the promise of [computerized testing] has yet to be fully realized. So far, when it has been applied, it has been used as a mechanical horse, not doing much more than could have been done with paper and pencil testing except that it is faster (a little) and more expensive (a lot)." We believe it is possible to do better, and the following is our plan.

In chapter 2, we situate our discussion in the context of new technologies that make it possible for choice to become the core of assessment (and not in the degraded sense of multiple-choice tests). We also provide an anchoring example of a computerized, choice-based assessment. In part II, we turn to theoretical matters to help unseat current beliefs about what we should be assessing. Chapter 3 maintains that choice is what most of the stakeholders in education care about, despite the fact that they often talk in terms of knowledge and skills. To make room for choice-based assessment, chapter 4 tries to clarify why knowledge-based assessments are a mismatch for the aims of education. The chapter highlights the fact that knowledge has not always been the frame of assessment and that the current emphasis on knowledge has made it difficult to connect assessments to outcomes beyond knowledge. Chapter 5 continues the argument by focusing on the static nature of knowledge assessments, and it offers an alternative model of a dynamic assessment that evaluates learning in action.

In part III, we turn to more practical matters. Chapter 6 provides several concrete cases of choice-based assessments that reveal what knowledge-based assessments cannot—for example, persistence after failure. Chapter 7 considers a related practical matter: twenty-first-century standards. The chapter supplies a pair of organizing frames that can integrate choice outcomes into standards while avoiding laundry lists of goals, which can leave assessment designers without guiding principles.

In part IV, we turn to matters of practice. We concentrate on the practice of designing assessments. Chapter 8 provides a brief tutorial on technical aspects of assessment, including constructs, validity, and reliability. Reliability, in particular, is problematic, because it presumes a stable construct, whereas education presupposes a trajectory of change. Chapter 9 contends that assessments would be more useful if we loosen the grip of some past approaches, so that assessments can be designed to evaluate learning experiences rather than just individual student achievement. Also, new computational developments make it possible to handle much more complex views of learning, but this depends on exploratory data mining as opposed to hypothesis testing. Chapter 10 lays out a research and development agenda for creating choice-based assessments. It includes the description of new platforms for democratizing and crowdsourcing the design and evaluation of assessments, along with several methodological strategies for making headway.

In part V, we turn to the most difficult aspect of assessment. Chapter 11 considers issues of fairness, where there is a delicate balance between encouraging and forcing good choices. In fact, before we move forward in our argument, we should clarify what we mean when we use the term *choice*. We take it as foundational that a primary goal of education is to help students develop aspirations and understandings so they can make choices that maximize their chances of succeeding within and beyond school, and we believe, therefore, that choice should be at the heart of assessment. Yet we recognize that not all choices are in the purview of education. Choice assessments should not be a backdoor way to enforce beliefs that fall outside the domain of publicly sponsored education (such as whether students make the "correct" choice about a political or religious matter). Instead, choice-based assessments should indicate whether students can learn and adapt in productive ways. Our discussion of choice-based assessments thus refers to learning-relevant choices such as how and what to learn, not all choices. Nevertheless, measuring choices—the stuff of agency and freedom—raises difficult questions about the province of education in shaping and assessing children. Choice-based assessments bring issues of fairness into helpful relief. Chapter 12 summarizes our argument.

2 Enter Technology

Many new technologies are about choice. When browsing the Web for information, each click can be considered a choice about learning. When deciding which online sources to trust and which friends to consult, people are making learning choices. When using scientific simulations, people make choices about sequences of settings that will yield the most telling results. There is a good match between current digital technologies and choice-based assessments. But we are getting ahead of ourselves. Before digging into the argument for choice as the interpretative framework for learning outcomes, we want to preview the general significance of technology for assessment. Digital technologies make it possible to teach and assess in new ways, and the lure of computerized efficiency can serve as a Trojan horse for delivering these new ways of teaching and assessing.

Historically, technology has always had a powerful influence on instruction and assessment. To take a remote example, the Dark Ages had limited technologies for information storage. Information therefore was carefully transmitted from teacher to pupil—a flame from one candle to the next. Monks painstakingly transcribed manuscripts letter for letter. One can imagine that assessments of monks largely involved their abilities to reproduce what came before without error, and a good deal of instruction also focused on errorless knowledge transmission.

The assessment enterprise has always been quick to adopt the efficiencies of new technologies—perhaps quicker than the instructional enterprise. Most people born before the twenty-first century are familiar with the no. 2 pencil and bubble forms. The bubble form was a technology that rapidly permeated the assessment enterprise. Professor Ben D. Wood, who helped design the bubble form and the IBM 805 that scored it, used the resulting income to endow graduate student fellowships at Teachers College, Columbia University. More recently, the bubble form has been replaced by fully automated computerized testing, which can collect, analyze, and transmit data the moment a test is over (or even sooner).

Ideally, in the rush to embrace more efficient assessment technologies, new forms of assessments can be introduced that influence education in productive ways. There is some evidence that this is already happening. As we describe next, there are technologies that embed assessments into instruction so that there is no need to "close the store to take inventory." There are also promising instances of technologies that can support non-linear curricula and assessment, so that students can make choices about what and how to learn.

These examples, which we describe below, all depend on large-scale environments that require many hours of interaction before any useful information can be gathered. To serve a broad range of goals, assessments need to be more nimble. And to show how this is possible, we conclude this chapter with an anchoring case of a digital choice-based assessment designed to assess critical thinking. It may not be what you expect in a test.

How New Technologies Can Remove Earlier Efficiency Constraints

Many assessment regimes are inefficient, because time spent on the test is not time spent on learning. One key improvement fashioned by technology is the ability to integrate assessment seamlessly into the process of learning itself. Cognitive tutors provide an excellent example (Koedinger and Anderson 1997). These programs monitor how students are solving problems on the computer. The assessments are embedded within the problem-solving tasks themselves. Much like a tutor observing how a pupil is solving a problem, the computer system adjusts the instruction based on a model of what the student can do so far. In this way, assessments can provide useful feedback to inform, rather than compete with, learning opportunities.

Another new way to implement assessments without displacing the time spent on learning is with video games. Good video games offer massive amounts of feedback that players can use to improve their performance, and the consequence of doing well is that new learning opportunities open up (e.g., by leveling up). James Gee (2003) has made the compelling case that video games are a great model for effective instruction and assessment. In good video games, assessment is an integral part of the design, and it is built into the core mechanics of the learning. David Shaffer (2006) further uses games to complement nonvirtual experiences, so it becomes possible to use the game as an assessment of the combined experiences.

A second important promise of technology is that it can alleviate management demands. The result of this promise is the possibility of nonlinear formats of instruction that allow for student exploration and choice about what as well as how to learn. To understand the significance of this development, it is crucial to appreciate what it can replace.

Currently, most classroom instruction follows a strict, predetermined linear sequence that precludes significant student choice about learning. School textbooks rarely ask students to choose how or what to learn, even when students are taking an elective course. The assumption is that these decisions should be left to experts, who can make more efficient learning choices than a novice could. There is merit to this assumption, but the price is too high when it removes all choice. For instance, the skill of time management cannot be taught effectively in schools where activities are regimented to the minute and enforced by bells. There are few opportunities for students to make choices and learn about time management in school. (Therefore, parents often use homework to teach their children time management in a context of learning.) Similarly, if students do not have opportunities to make choices about learning, they will not learn how to choose well (unless they gain such experiences through informal learning).

A predetermined linear curriculum helps to avert the challenge of monitoring many different learning trajectories. High school teachers can have roughly 150 students per day, which means teachers could face the prospect of tracking 150 different learning trajectories. It is much easier to track the position of each student against a single trajectory as specified by the curriculum. Even in the context of individualized computer instruction, it has been common to assume a single, idealized trajectory. The cognitive tutors, like all forms of programmed instruction, presuppose an ordered sequence of learning, so it is possible to keep track of students and then move them forward or backward in the sequence depending on their performance.

Newer genres of technologies make it possible to forego a linear progression without a concomitant loss of efficiency in learning or management. They provide for learner choice while still supplying ample opportunities for assessment and learning.

Multiplayer video games like *World of Warcraft* (http://us.battle.net/wow/en) include a slate of choices about what to do, whom to be, what to learn, and how to learn. Here is a sample of the choices available to new players of the *World of Warcraft* at the time of this writing (more options are added frequently). Players choose one of over two hundred Realms in which to create their characters (there are four different types of Realm, determined by whether or not players are expected to act "in character," and whether or not players are allowed to attack each other). They then choose one of two factions (Alliance or Horde), one of ten species (Blood Elves, Draenei, Humans, etc.), one of two genders (male or female), and one of ten careers (Druid, Hunter, Shaman, etc.). The players must then choose their appearances from among thousands of possible configurations—and all this is before the game has even begun.

Once the players bring their characters into the world, they choose their professions, talents, friends, enemies, quests, worldviews, and goals. They then embark on an open-ended adventuring career. Everything that *World of Warcraft* players learn about how to succeed in the game (which is a lot—it is a complex game) is defined by their choices, from the game's setup to whom they interact with online. This profusion of choices might seem daunting, but it encourages players to feel a real ownership and become strongly invested in their characters' success.

Despite the nonlinear format, with players choosing their trajectories, these types of choice-rich environments are filled with assessments. *World of Warcraft* is instrumented with extremely refined metrics of player preferences, progress, and strengths. There are metrics that indicate various powers along with levels of accomplishment and access. These metrics are clearly available to players through gauges, points, game levels, ratings by peers, and so forth. They serve as powerful motivators to do even better (Reeves and Read 2009). In this case, assessment and learning are built into an environment of high choice.

Nimble Assessments

The cognitive tutor and full-blown video games are too bulky for most assessment purposes. There are advantages to making smaller and more nimble environments for assessment. First, nimble assessments do not depend on students completing many hours of a complex game or instructional sequence before it is possible to make any useful assessments.

Second, smaller assessments can target specific choices by their design. This is quite different from searching for diagnostic patterns amid the millions of possible choice combinations in larger open environments.

Third, building smaller choice-based assessments can be within the reach of many, thereby potentially helping to increase the democratization of assessment design. As we describe later, with the right resources, we can make it so that members of the "public" can work on designing their own choice-based assessments.

Fourth, multiple smaller assessments make it possible to assess the same constellation of choices using several measures instead of just one. The results from a single, monolithic assessment are questionable, because they may be due to unknown peculiarities of the environment. By using multiple assessments, it is possible to mitigate these concerns by showing the generalization of student behaviors across multiple environments.

Finally, there is value to having an assessment that can be used to compare different learning experiences. In the cases of video games, the cognitive tutor, and many embedded assessments, the assessments are locked into a specific model of instruction and delivery system. It is oftentimes useful to have assessments that stand independently of a specific instructional package, so that it is possible to use the assessment to compare the effectiveness of different instructional models and learning experiences.

An Example of a Choice-Based Assessment

A modest illustration of a nimble, choice-based assessment comes from our work on *choicelets*. Choicelets take the form of short and (hopefully) engaging games that students want to complete. To complete the game, each choicelet requires some learning, and we keep a log of students' choices relevant to that learning. Different choicelets are designed to assess specific constellations of choices relevant to learning.

In the current example, we describe a game called *Ohno! Has Talent*. The game takes the form of a talent show. It is designed to measure critical thinking. Critical thinking is the process by which people decide what to believe (Norris 1985). Most assessments of critical thinking evaluate reasoning—for instance, the ability to recognize when assumptions do not lead to conclusions. Critical thinking assessments are rarely connected to learning outcomes. From this narrow vantage point, critical thinking gets confused with (deductive) problem solving, on the one hand, and brute intelligence, on the other. Here are two examples of items drawn from a practice packet for a standardized test of critical thinking (Watson and Glaser 2002). One can see that they measure decontextualized deductive reasoning—something of the sort that lawyers might use on a case that has been handed to them.

I. Statement: ***The proper aim of education in a free society is to prepare the individual to make wise decisions.*** **Which of the following assumptions are made in the statement?**

1. People educated in a free society will not make unwise decisions (Yes/No).
2. Some education systems in our society do not have the proper aim (Yes/No).
3. Some kinds of education can help individuals make wise decisions (Yes/No).
4. In a society that is not free, the individual cannot make any decisions (Yes/No).

II. Statement: ***No responsible leader can avoid making difficult decisions. Some responsible leaders dislike making difficult decisions.***
Therefore:

1. Some decisions are distasteful to some people (Yes/No).
2. Irresponsible leaders avoid things they dislike (Yes/No).
3. Some responsible leaders do things they dislike doing (Yes/No).

We thought it might be useful to recast critical thinking in a choice-based assessment and regain the broader meaning of critical thinking as the process of deciding what to believe. Therefore, we assessed the choice to engage in critical thinking for the purpose of learning. As will become evident, there are a number of differences between our assessment and the critical thinking items above. The choice-based assessment, for example, occurs in the context of a game on learning about color mixing. Making assessments fun should be useful for those who would like to examine the effects of informal learning experiences, where it can be difficult to ask visiting learners to complete tests and surveys. Leaving a museum with a test is not compelling, but leaving with a pointer to a set of free games could be.

Figure 2.1 (plate 1) shows the main interface of the *Ohno! Has Talent* assessment. There are three contestants, who each sing a song. The contestants want the overhead lights to beam specific colors when they are singing. The students' task is to mix the primary light colors to make the contestants' preferred color beams. Students use the little color buttons near the bottom of the figure to mix the light. The music bars just above the buttons show the colors that a contestant would like. After the

Figure 2.1 (Plate 1)

Ohno! Has Talent: An example of a choice-based assessment for critical thinking

Students mix the stage lights to shine colors when the contestants sing. The contestant Otter wanted an orange beam, and the student correctly set the color lights at the bottom to make orange. Most students know about mixing primary colors for paint (subtractive color), but light depends on a different set of primary colors (additive color). To learn the rules of additive color, students have an experiment room in the upper-right corner, and they have a set of catalogs that show different color-mixing results, some of which are subtractive charts and some of which are additive charts. Do students choose to engage in critical thinking by deciding what charts to believe?

students have set the lights for a contestant, the contestant sings. As the song progresses, the stage light shines the color that comes from the combination of lights the student picked. If the students mixed correctly, the singer receives stars for the song, and if they mixed poorly, the singer does poorly. There are three rounds, and in each one, the color mixing becomes more challenging. Figure 2.1 (plate 1) depicts the final round for contestant Otter. For the last part of his song Otter wanted orange, and the student has mixed correctly by choosing two red lights and one green light. Children play the game in ten to twenty minutes, and so far, they find it quite entertaining.

Most children have been taught that the primary colors are red, yellow, and blue. The primary colors for mixing light, however, are red, *green,* and blue. The RGB input of a television refers to these primary colors. Red and green make yellow, and hence red, green, and red make orange. A major part of the game involves learning about mixing light.

To help students learn, the digital environment includes a pair of resources. On the upper-right portion of the screen is an experiment room, where students can try out different color combinations without risking a wrong answer for a contestant. On the lower-right side, there is a faux shopping catalog. Different companies sell charts for mixing colors. Some of the charts are for subtractive color, and some are for additive color. Figure 2.1 (plate 1) shows the chart that sets out the correct additive color combinations and their results. Students have to use critical thinking to decide which charts to believe, if they choose to use the charts at all. To make our assessment, we track the students' choices in log files generated by the game.

In an initial study using a similar environment with sixth-grade children, the results were quite clear. Children who chose to look at the catalog of charts learned much more about mixing additive color than their counterparts did. More important, these same children were also doing better in school. In fact, the amount of time students committed to figuring out the catalog entries predicted about 35 percent of the variation in the students' grades in their mathematics classes (the only classes for which we had records). While all the students seemed happy to play the game, those who chose not to engage in critical thinking were also the students who were doing worse in mathematics. The 35 percent level of prediction is high, especially considering that *Ohno! Has Talent* has little to do with solving math problems as they appear on the children's mathematics tests. The assessment captured something crucial about how these children go about learning that is affecting their success in mathematics—and will likely do so in the future.

This choicelet example, which is only promissory pending further research, offers two take-home messages. First, by assessing students' choices during learning, we can discover a great deal about the processes they do or do not use to learn. Ideally, with this choice-based information, we can help students to make better choices for learning. The second point is that we can assess choices that are critical to learning but that are missed by most tests. Tracking the process of learning is different from simply detecting whether a student knows an answer or not, which is the output of most tests. Choice-based assessments can provide a much richer corpus of information from which to draw actionable information about learners. We can locate the source of the problem rather than just the consequence. The students who were doing the worst in math class, for instance, were those who used the experiment room to solve each problem through trial and error. These students, instead of trying to develop an overall understanding of additive color, were simply attempting to get the right answer for each problem in turn. In the best case, identifying this pattern of *malchoices* can help a teacher address the underlying learning issue, which is that the students are trying to solve each problem in turn rather than discovering the general principle that governs the solutions to all problems.

Summary

With more choices and interactivity comes more information about the learner. Performance assessments, such as portfolio and project-based assessments, have tried to capitalize on the increased information found in choice-rich environments (e.g., Resnick and Resnick 1994). Richard Shavelson, Gail Baxter, and Jerome Pine (1991), for example, describe a kit-based performance assessment for science. Students conduct physical experiments to determine which brand of paper towel absorbs more water. The assessment provides information about the students' abilities (or inclinations) to use experimental logic and take careful measurements. Unfortunately, the authors also point out that performance assessments can be prohibitively expensive to deploy and score at scale.

Technology can help overcome the difficulties associated with increased information. Computers can deliver assessments where students make choices about how to learn, and the computers can automatically log all user behaviors that might be of interest to a teacher, assessor, or researcher, ranging from chat logs to virtual interpersonal distance to direction of gaze. It is an ethnographer's thick description for free. Computers provide new efficiencies that make tractable what was once impracticable. And with new empirical capabilities, new theories are sure to follow, as we will now discuss.

II Theoretical Matters

3 Choice Is the Central Concern

For the many stakeholders in education, choice is the central concern. Parents care about their children's choices, such as how they spend their free time, whether they try hard at school, and even whether they develop a sense of the possibilities from which they might choose. Parents hope for "good choices," and arguably, many parents care about "good knowledge" (or grades) to the extent that it enables opportunities for choices later on. Yet despite the manifest importance of choice, current assessments primarily evaluate a degraded sense of choice, as in choosing an answer on a multiple-choice test, or choosing to opt out of a test or school altogether.

Educators also value choice. In most primary school classrooms, there are charts on the wall that specify the top classroom priorities, and the top entry is usually "Make Good Choices." Educators want schools to help students choose and learn once they leave school. Daniel Schwartz, John Bransford, and David Sears (2005) interviewed school superintendents to determine what help learning scientists might provide to their endeavor. One possibility was that the superintendents would ask for assistance in achieving high test scores to increase their districts' standings. They did not. Instead, "the surprisingly unanimous answer (they were surprised as well) was that they wanted us to help students make their own choices in the future. They wanted the students to be able to 'learn for themselves' and make informed decisions. They believed that well-designed school experiences could transfer to help children continue to learn once they left school" (ibid., 2).

Subsequent discussions with school principals revealed a similar concern. The principals often explained that they recognized the value of the yearly high-stakes tests and wanted their students to do well. But they also wanted assessments that could help them evaluate how they were achieving many of their local educational goals. These goals invariably map onto student choices—for example, students' love of learning, critical thinking, and willingness to collaborate well. Ideally, assessments would provide information to superintendents and principals about how their schools are doing in these respects, but measurement of such outcomes is beyond the reach of mainstream assessment practices.

Educational researchers also care about choice. Erna Yackel and Paul Cobb (1996, 473) nicely summarize the perspective of many: "The development of intellectual and social autonomy is a major goal in the current educational reform movement, more generally, and in the reform movement in mathematics education, in particular. In this regard, the reform is in agreement with Piaget that the main purpose of education is autonomy." The central component of autonomy, of course, is the ability to make and execute choices.

When one looks at the terms used in many debates (and education has many debates), they appear to have choice at their core, even if the debate is framed in other terms (e.g., constructivism versus direct instruction). Table 3.1 provides a sampling of opposite positions. The left side shows the terms adopted by reform-minded educators, and the right side displays the terms they use to label the alternatives. We assume that the preference for greater choice reflects a desire for students to develop agency. Choice is what creates the possibility of agency, and therefore many educational researchers prefer high-choice environments for learning.

Unfortunately, when it comes to justifying the practical outcomes of their theories and instruction, researchers often rely on gains in knowledge, because knowledge is the accepted frame for what it means to have learned. It would be more harmonious if these agency-driven theories used choice as the outcome of education rather than only knowledge. A focus on knowledge can sometimes be incommensurate with choice. Sigmund Tobias

Table 3.1
Contrasts in educational discourse often tacitly appeal to a notion of agency

High choice	Low choice
Student centered	Teacher centered
Student voice	Authoritarian
Elective	Compulsory
Participatory	Assembly line
Active	Passive
Discovery	Programmed instruction
Constructivism	Direct instruction

(2009, 343), for example, concludes that "student choice may be a confounding variable" in research on student learning. In this view, choice is a nuisance variable to be controlled. By controlling choice, it would be possible to infer the mechanical gears that drive knowledge acquisition. If people were only like blocks on inclined planes, researchers would not have to worry about choice when evaluating knowledge acquisition.

Informal educators also care about choice (e.g., Falk and Dierking 2002). Informal learning is frequently self-selected, and thus it has been taken as a setting of high relevance to outcomes of interest, identity, and participation. The 2009 National Research Council report, *Learning Science in Informal Environments*, added two strands to the original four strands of science learning established by the 2007 report, *Taking Science to School*. Specifically, it included "strands 1 and 6—which are of special value in informal learning environments" (Bell, Lewenstein, Shouse, and Feder, 2009). Strand 1 refers to interest, excitement, and motivation in science, and strand 6 relates to identification with science. These new strands emphasize the importance of students developing an attraction toward science so they will make choices to engage in it. Robert Tai, Christine Liu, Adam Maltese, and Xitao Fan (2006), for example, found that science career aspirations in eighth grade are a better predictor of later science engagement than class grades. To measure these new strands of outcomes, we need new types of assessments that go beyond the knowledge-driven curriculum tests so prevalent in formal learning settings. And simply asking students to check off their interests and motivations in a survey has insufficient precision for most purposes.

Outside of instruction, the need to make learning choices is the norm. These choices are where the rubber of school meets the road of life. One especially vivid case involves preparation for the bar exam. Law school graduates need to pass a bar exam to become practicing lawyers, but law schools typically do not teach the specific knowledge needed for the exam. Law schools focus on broad issues and ways of thinking versus the specifics of particular state codes. To prepare for the exam, students routinely take special courses independent of law school. These preparation courses provide an overabundance of learning resources such as readings, reviews, outlines, practice tests, case synopses, videos, live lectures, workshops, and online tutorials. Figure 3.1 shows the thousands of pages of textual materials for one such course, the California BARBRI (http://www.barbri.com). Across materials, the content is highly redundant, so rather than plowing through everything, well-educated law students choose the presentation format, activities, and timing of their study as well as the social arrangements that they feel suit their learning needs for different topics within the curriculum. Their learning is driven by their choices of what, when, how, and with whom to learn.

In this example, experiences within law school help students make sense of the content of the materials in order to make choices about how to navigate the mountain of resources to optimize their progress toward the exam. Of course, not everyone has to prepare for a bar exam, but everyone faces situations outside of school for which school knowledge is not enough, such as comparing cars or camcorders. In these instances, the choices that people make about how to learn will determine their success.

Figure 3.1

Some of the study materials for the BARBRI course that law students take to prepare for the California Bar Examination

The BARBRI course includes a massive collection of learning resources from books and practice tests to videotapes, lectures, and group sessions. Ideally, law school prepares students to choose how and what to learn from the mountain of materials.

The modern workplace also puts choice at a premium. In prior generations, people could often anticipate a clear career trajectory and stable lifetime employment with one firm. In today's economy, jobs are no longer stable, and skills need to be updated frequently. New information and affiliated technologies appear daily, and workers must constantly adapt to new contexts, colleagues, jobs, and even careers to keep up with changes in competition as well as industry structure (Benner 2002). In addition, workers are expected to participate in their own growth, as demonstrated by the widespread use of continuous improvement programs across industries where the retooling of skills is considered part of the job itself (Appelbaum and Batt 1994). At every level, the ability to accomplish difficult tasks in the present-day economy is more likely to depend on one's ability to navigate the vast array of informational resources than one's grasp of static knowledge that could be measured by today's assessments. The question is no longer, "What do you know?" It is now, "What can you successfully choose to learn?"

Finally, choice is at the center of a free society that stresses democracy and opportunity. Democracy depends on people's abilities to recognize and execute choices within the constraints that make society possible. Agency and participation are operationalized in choice. Questions of identity and inclusion matter because they contribute to the choices that people make.

Societies achieve their ideals of choice to varying degrees because of preexisting conditions, biases, and ill-formed social structures. Schools should not further contribute to a loss of choice; instead, they should directly address issues of choice in developmentally appropriate ways. For obvious reasons, children should not have the same freedom of choice as adults. At the same time, choice is at the center of our social philosophy, and therefore should be at the center of assessments that are increasingly the beacon of what schools should accomplish.

4 The Isolation of Knowledge

Before continuing the positive case for choice-based assessments, we will now consider the negative one against the current state of affairs—namely, knowledge-based assessments. As a topic of inquiry and debate, the "concept" of knowledge has fueled great advances in scholarship, but it is not ideal for achieving the practical and normative aims of education. To mention just one shortcoming, knowledge assessments are inherently retrospective, but past knowledge is a small slice of what matters. Current knowledge assessments miss critical factors relevant to learning such as motivations to learn, responses to feedback and change, tacit understandings, and abilities to learn when no longer being told what to do.

Some readers might object that choice measurement is simply new packaging for knowledge assessment, because people's knowledge largely determines their choices. We agree that knowledge is *one* important determinant of choice, but this objection mistakes the purpose of assessment as being scientific rather than normative and practical. The scientific challenge would be to explain people's choices, and people's knowledge would surely be one causal component of such an explanation.

Education, however, is first and foremost a practical matter, and as such, its lead paradigm of measurement should be the one closest to the realm of action. At the end of the day, whether a student has "good knowledge" will be crucial only to the degree that knowledge leads to good choices, so why not measure choices directly in educational assessments? In the meantime, scientific efforts can continue to see if a rational, knowledge-based account can provide a sufficient explanation of choice, which we highly doubt given the centrality of emotion in choice (see Damasio 1994).

There is instrumental value to using knowledge-based assessments. Measuring what a student knows can help a great deal in deciding what to do next during instruction. The skills that come from knowledge are also essential for repetitive tasks; for example, it is important to ensure that people know how to drive a car before they get a license. Nevertheless, knowledge-based assessments have such a stronghold on the public mind that they obscure the point of it all. We therefore will play the devil's advocate and mount a one-sided argument to help dethrone knowledge (and the skills it enables) as the central assessed outcome of education. Knowledge is simply too narrow, and we believe that we can capture most knowledge-based constructs using choice-based assessments anyway.

We need to be honest here. We are cognitive scientists who attempt to formalize the nature of knowledge along with its implications for learning and problem solving (e.g., Schwartz and Black 1996). We use theories of knowledge acquisition to design our instruction, and we use theories of knowledge to help design measures for scientific experiments. We also believe that good knowledge yields good outcomes. To paraphrase Socrates: knowing the Good yields doing the Good. Knowledge can also be its own reward independent of any utility. Appreciating a piece of art or recognizing the elegance of a mathematical proof does not require an instrumental justification. Even rote memory has its pleasures, as demonstrated by the surprising satisfaction of simply remembering a fact when watching a television quiz show. These things do not need to be justified for their practical outcomes. We once had a conversation with a music professor who wished he was doing more important research on math and science learning. We pointed out that people spend much more time listening to music than doing algebra. We asked what could be more important than studying how to help people produce and appreciate it more. But as much as we love knowledge, and as much as we wish we had more of it, knowledge is a mismatch for the practical aims of assessment. Assessment is about shaping the direction of society and its members.

As we build our leverage to pry assessment from the grasp of knowledge, it may be useful to recognize that knowledge has not always been the focus of assessment. Assessment in the United States has had many purposes, ranging from student tracking to individualized instruction to program evaluation to holding schools accountable (Haertel and Herman 2005). The purposes and methods of assessment can change, and we propose that now is a good time to change again, given the advent of new technologies and methods. Early on, assessment attempted to measure intelligence. Alfred Binet's original goal in developing the first intelligence test was to help teachers objectively identify children who needed special considerations. This approach failed as a model of assessment across education, in part because it confused purportedly unchangeable individual differences with contextual sources of group variability, including culture and socioeconomic status. Subsequent behaviorist approaches measured performance. These approaches emphasized the decomposition and mastery of observable skills, and were an advance in that they focused on what people learned rather than traits that predetermined learning. The behavioral assessments, however, were training oriented and too narrow to help evaluate whether students were being prepared for life beyond the specific tasks. More recently, cognitive approaches have concentrated on assessing knowledge.

Knowledge assessments are an improvement over training and intelligence tests because they are more flexible. Knowledge assessments assume that adding more knowledge is possible, unlike intelligence tests. And unlike behaviorist assessments, knowledge-based ones can also examine sources of learner confusion and do not require performance on a narrowly described set of trained tasks. Despite the relative value of knowledge-based assessments, the construct of knowledge has limitations that have hampered further advances. For example, knowledge is often conceptualized as a sort of "mental text," so instructional metaphors frequently suggest (incorrectly) that teaching is something like transmitting the text from the mind of the instructor into the mind of the learner, much like the monks transcribed letters from one volume to the next. With choice as the central construct, it becomes harder to develop simplistic and potentially ineffective metaphors like this one.

There is also a deeper set of theoretical problems that make knowledge problematic in the context of assessment. They all stem from the isolation of knowledge: it is isolated from the bulk of social science research; as a description of a mental state, it is isolated from context; and perhaps worst of all, as an organization of information, it is isolated from the rest of the person. We detail these issues next. In the following chapter, we explain a less theoretical problem with knowledge assessments: they measure problem solving and not learning.

Isolation from Social Sciences

When considering human behavior, most social sciences focus on choice rather than knowledge. Economics, for instance, examines how financial matters drive choice and vice versa. Sociology looks at how patterns of association and structure influence choice. Management sciences explore "social selection"—how employees choose to configure their tasks and social relations. Political science and philosophy are intimately concerned with the balance of choice and necessity. In *The Social Contract,* Jean-Jacques Rousseau ([1762] 1947 bk. I, chap. 6) puts freedom of choice as the fundamental issue: "The problem is to find a form of association . . . in which each, while uniting himself with all, may still obey himself alone, and remain as free as before."

This isolation of knowledge from other forms of scholarship comes at a loss to the field of assessment. For example, game theory, which examines choice behavior directly, could be a powerful source of ideas, but it has not been integrated into the discussion of assessment. Moreover, a focus on individual knowledge makes it difficult to develop joint accounts of both individual outcomes and social configurations that support learning. The language of knowledge theories and that of social theories do not readily make contact. States provide reports of student performance broken out by school. The reports indicate how the students at the school are scoring on average. If your child's school is doing poorly, you want to take action. Unfortunately, the knowledge tests are based on what students have in their head. So you have discovered that your child's school is not doing a great job, but there is nothing in the assessment that suggests what you might do on the social plane to help improve the state of affairs. This is because an assessment of knowledge is not an assessment of processes, and what you care about in classrooms is the process, not whether there is "knowledge in the air." We return to this point in chapter 9, on new types of process assessments.

In some cases, scholars do use knowledge, or the lack thereof, to help explain the choices that people make (e.g., Tversky and Kahneman 1974), but knowledge is only properly a means to an end. The goal in the social sciences is to account for human behavior, which is made manifest in choices. Treating knowledge as the primary outcome has left assessment as an isolated minority.

While it is beyond the scope of a book on assessment, it is not hard to envision how a theory of learning could be organized within choice. For instance, we can borrow from the search space formalism of Allen Newell and Herbert Simon (1972). The formalism creates something like a tree structure of possible states, whether they have actually occurred or not (e.g., an X in the middle of a tic-tac-toe board, an X in the lower-right corner, an O in the upper-left corner, and an O in the upper-right corner, and so on). The links among the states indicate possible pathways that lead from one state to another (e.g., add an X btween the two Os). The formalism proposes that reasoning is the process of searching through the paths in the tree structure to find the best path to achieve a final goal state (e.g., three Xs in a row).

To convert this scheme to handle choices, there would be three primary components: the context of choices, the choices taken, and the choices that are subsequently enabled. The context of choice is a specification of the field of learning choices that are available to a learner (i.e., possible states). Theories that focus on "positioning," for instance, would specify how authority relations determine the learning choices that are legitimated and available for a child or group of children (Harré and van Langenhove 1999). The second is a specification of the choices that learners actually make (i.e., traversal through the tree). Students may have dispositions or identifications toward some choices over others (Gresalfi 2009). They may perceive restricted agency and miss choice possibilities. And they may simply not notice the availability of some choices or make choices that are suboptimal for their own goals. Finally, the third component is how a taken choice affects subsequent choice options (i.e., possible next states). Some choices open doors, and others close them. How one choice affects future possible choices is a critical component that has been undertheorized in learning. Given the choice space, one can then start to theorize what shapes the field of choices; what explains the decisions that students, teachers, or any individual or group of learners make; and how specific configurations of choices open (or close) future opportunities for decision making about learning.

Isolation from Context

A second problem with knowledge, as typically formulated, is that it is isolated from context. Knowledge is a description of the mental contents of an individual. In one extreme formulation, conceptual knowledge is said to improve by an increase in the abstractness of the mental representations. The logic is that more abstract knowledge can apply to a broader set of situations because it is not tied to any single situation. According to this line of thinking, abstractness develops by a process of subtraction, so that less and less of the original context of learning appears in the knowledge. Some scholars, in fact, have proposed that knowledge should be taught as abstractly as possible to shortcut the deleterious effects of context-specific representations (Kaminski, Sloutsky, and Heckler 2008).

James Gibson and Elizabeth Gibson (1955) highlighted the irony of the abstraction-as-subtraction perspective. They pointed out that by this account, learning leads one farther from the world rather than closer to it, which seems absurd given that experts are much more able to perceive contextual information than are novices (e.g., a sommelier can taste differences among red wines that a novice would miss; see also Beiderman and Shiffrar 1987).

At the core of many intuitive and formal knowledge accounts is the idea that knowledge is a highly structured, internal representation or copy of experience—a well-organized picture or text in the head, to put it coarsely. But there are alternatives to mental representation for describing competent performance. Plato, for example, proposed that understanding is like the sun: it illuminates the world rather than copying it. So as opposed to looking for people's memories of specific facts, one needs to look at the processes by which people illuminate the facts as they arise. As a second analogy, take the case of a radio. The radio does not have a copy of the music it plays. Instead, it resonates to the context of the radio signals. If a radio could learn, it would not do so by constructing knowledge of the content it plays. It would get better at tuning more channels, separating one signal from another—in other words, learning would equate with better sensitivities for picking up and responding to contextual information. In both of these cases, knowledge does not copy experience, and the idea of looking for people's knowledge as a stand-alone representation does not make sense. As the literature on the transfer of learning from one setting to another has repeatedly demonstrated, learned behavior cannot be fully dissociated from the contexts of its acquisition or application (e.g., Barnett and Ceci 2002).

In knowledge-based assessments, context does not receive as much attention as it should. Most of education uses "supply-side" assessments, which test students on what was supplied by the curriculum. Because supply-side assessments are confined to the curriculum context, they run the risk of producing a self-tightening knot. If students do poorly on the assessment, instruction will increasingly start to look like the assessment itself—educators will teach to the test.

An alternative is a "demand-side" assessment. Here, the assessment is tethered to the demands of a future context rather than the past curriculum. The Programme for International Student Assessment (PISA) is a demand-side international assessment that is being increasingly used by policymakers (http://www.pisa.oecd.org). The items on the PISA reflect the demands of the work world. The PISA has a framework that specifies knowledge competencies (e.g., multistep problem solving) and domains of application (e.g., math), and there is a good deal of heated negotiation among nations and scholars about which facts and skills should be included in the PISA test. Despite its merits in considering the future context of knowledge application, the PISA still suffers from a lack of attention to the context created by the assessment items themselves. Construction of the specific items on the test—the contextual vehicle of the assessment—is often farmed out to "item makers" and taken as nonproblematic. Multiple-choice, true/false, or free-response items are all acceptable as long as they are efficient, reliable indicators of competency within the domain. If the PISA used choice as its main construct, then context could not be an afterthought in an assessment item, because choice does not exist independently of the decision-making context.

We believe assessments should not be confined to knowledge but rather should include choice. At the same time, the choice constructs need to be tied to contexts. In the *Ohno! Has Talent* example in chapter 2, it would be inaccurate to say that we measured "critical thinking." It is better to say we measured "critical thinking in a context of implicitly conflicting information sources." The degree to which we will need to contextualize the choice assessments when summarizing their results is an empirical question versus an assumption. It may ultimately have to be "critical thinking about implicitly conflicting information sources among chart products," or worse, "critical thinking about implicitly conflicting information sources among chart products when solving puzzles about mixing light." Hopefully, the choice-based contexts will not have to be so narrowly defined that there is an overproliferation of assessments. But acknowledging the significance of context is important in order to move beyond the mistaken assumption that what assessments measure is context-free knowledge.

Isolation from the Rest of a Person

A third reason to relax the hold of knowledge on assessment is that knowledge is isolated from the rest of the individual. Across the history of *Cognitive Science,* a premier interdisciplinary journal focusing on knowledge, it is hard to find more than a handful of articles on motivation, emotion, or identity. The fact that *Cognitive Science* partitions human performance by considering "cold knowledge" and excluding "hot affect" makes some sense. There is scientific value to analytically separating systems that nevertheless work together in nature. The study of knowledge as a separate assembly has led to great advances in psychology, philosophy, and computer science, to mention just a few areas of success. The primary goal of assessment, however, is the improvement of learning. To achieve this goal, it is important to include all sources of information about an individual's learning, not just cognitive markers of "cold" thinking.

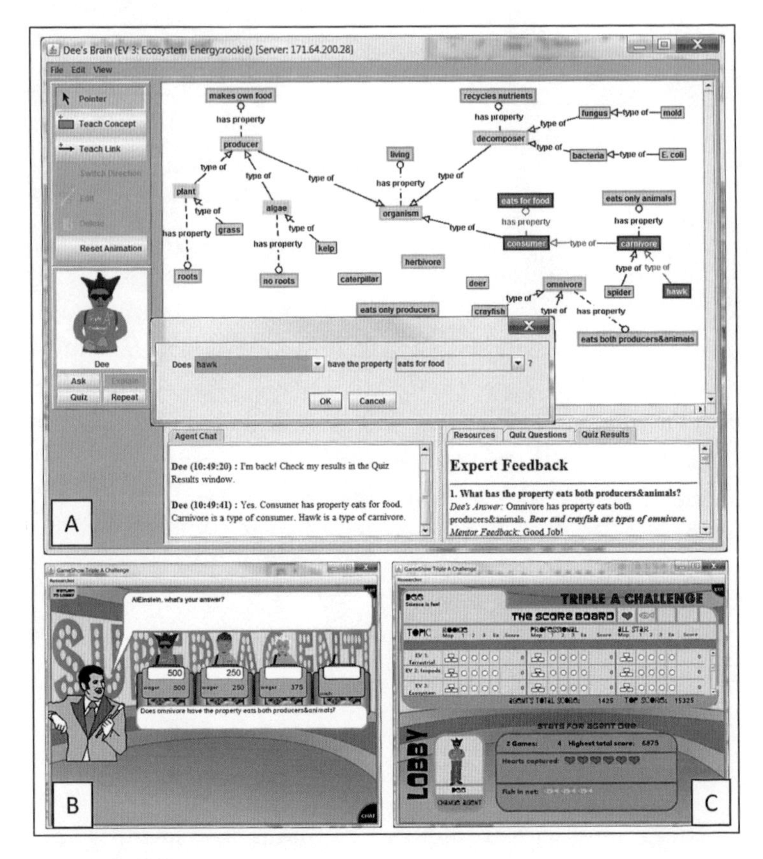

Figure 4.1 (Plate 2)

Teachable Agent environment

(a) The student has named her agent "Dee," customized Dee's look, and taught her about consumers, producers, and decomposers. Dee has answered the question posed by the student, "Does a hawk eat food?" both graphically and in text, by chaining from hawk to carnivore to consumer to eat food. (b) Students can have their agents play an online game, where the students wager on whether their agent will give the right answer. The students can also chat online with one another. (c) The Lobby is the main entry portal into the environment. It includes the various assignments for the agent plus access to customizing features, reading resources, the agent teaching interface, chatting, and the online game.

Consider the case of low-achieving students. A knowledge assessment points out that they do not have strong knowledge. But ideally, an assessment would help predict what choices would lead to better learning, and what contexts would help promote those choices. Catherine Chase, Doris Chin, Marily Oppezzo, and Daniel Schwartz (2009) conducted a study that examined learner choices. Students worked with an intelligent software environment called a Teachable Agent (http://workingexamples.org/frontend/project/18). Figure 4.1 (plate 2) shows the main teaching interface of the software. In this environment, students make digital concept maps under the guise of creating the Teachable Agent's brain. The digital maps are interactive and can use simple artificial intelligence techniques to answer questions by chaining through their links and nodes. The environment includes quizzes for the agents—a game show where the agents and their teachers (students) can chat, share reading resources, and play for hearts and fish.

In the teaching condition, the students were told that by creating a concept map, they were teaching a computer character (a Teachable Agent) to answer questions. The map was the agent's brain, and the character in the lower-left corner represented the agent that the students were teaching. In the self condition, the students were told they were simply making a concept map to help themselves learn (there was no cover story of the map being an agent's brain). They thought they were just using a "smart" program, and the character in the lower-left corner stood for themselves.

On a posttest of learning, the teaching condition outperformed the self condition. When separating students based on their prior achievement, low-achieving students in the teaching condition performed as well as the high-achieving students in the self condition, and they did much better than the low-achieving students in the self condition. It is hard to explain these differences by appealing to differences in the low-achieving students' knowledge in the two conditions, either beforehand or afterward. After all, they were low knowledge to start with. Instead, the key assessment involved examining students' choices of whether and how to learn. The logs from their use of the software revealed what happened. The low-achieving teaching students did well because they chose to spend more time working on their maps; they read the relevant resources more and edited their maps' links and nodes in accordance. In contrast, the low-achieving students in the self condition spent more of their time chatting and playing the available game.

One might wonder what psychological states led to the choices. This is a good question that the researchers subsequently addressed (the Teachable Agent created an ego-protective buffer plus a sense of responsibility, so students did not feel bad about mistakes but instead were compelled to figure out how to fix them). As we mentioned previously, though, this is a scientific question indifferent to the assessment of learning choices.

How far can assessments go by focusing on choice, without positing knowledge to explain those choices? This is an open question. The purpose of this book is to catalyze exploration of this question such that the field of assessment can move beyond cold knowledge assessments that are so isolated they cannot evaluate student motivations in the context of learning.

Plate 1 (Figure 2.1)

Ohno! Has Talent: An example of a choice-based assessment for critical thinking

Students mix the stage lights to shine colors when the contestants sing. The contestant Otter wanted an orange beam, and the student correctly set the color lights at the bottom to make orange. Most students know about mixing primary colors for paint (subtractive color), but light depends on a different set of primary colors (additive color). To learn the rules of additive color, students have an experiment room in the upper-right corner, and they have a set of catalogs that show different color-mixing results, some of which are subtractive charts and some of which are additive charts. Do students choose to engage in critical thinking by deciding what charts to believe?

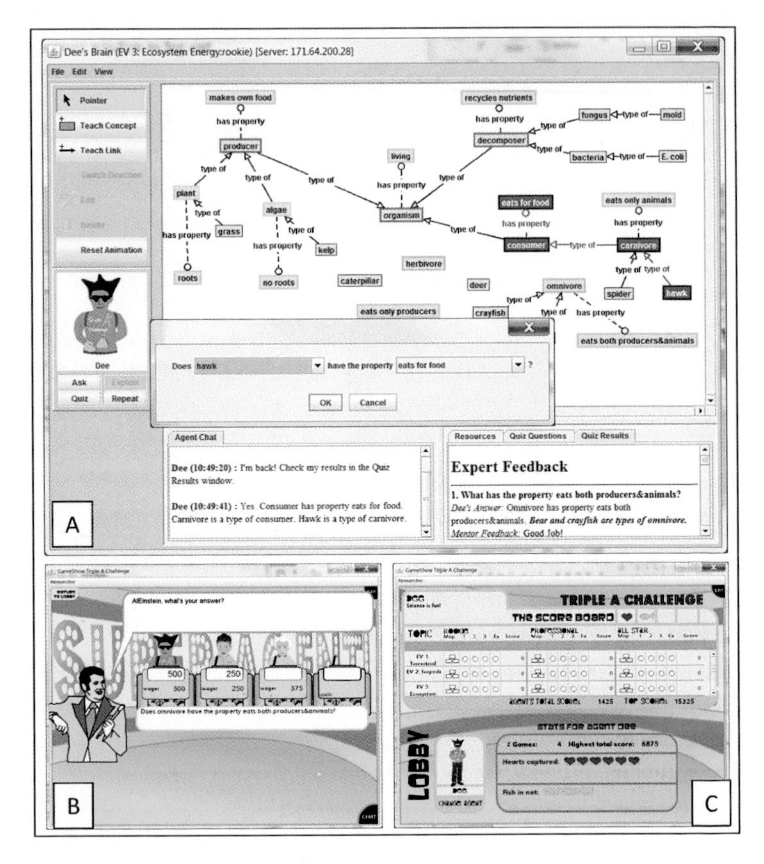

Plate 2 (Figure 4.1)

Teachable Agent environment

(a) The student has named her agent "Dee," customized Dee's look, and taught her about consumers, producers, and decomposers. Dee has answered the question posed by the student, "Does a hawk eat food?" both graphically and in text, by chaining from hawk to carnivore to consumer to eat food. (b) Students can have their agents play an online game, where the students wager on whether their agent will give the right answer. The students can also chat online with one another. (c) The Lobby is the main entry portal into the environment. It includes the various assignments for the agent plus access to customizing features, reading resources, the agent teaching interface, chatting, and the online game.

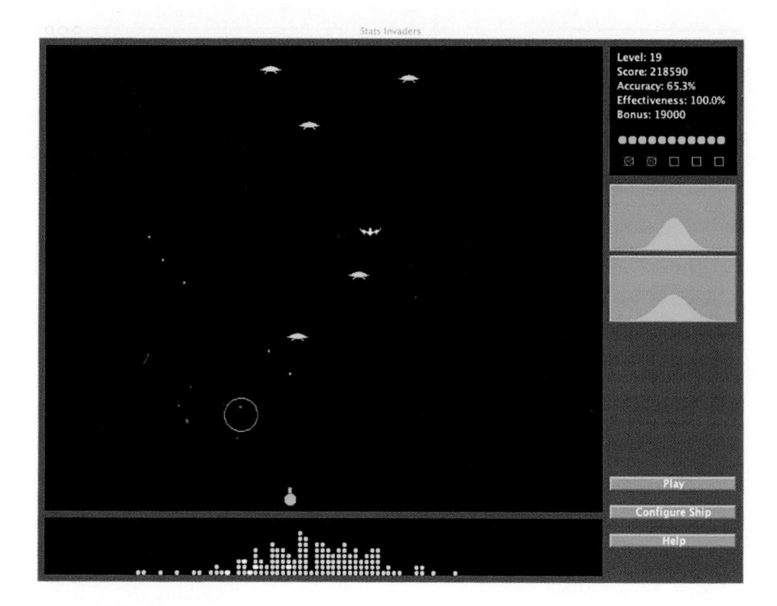

Plate 3 (Figure 5.2)

Stats Invaders: A video game to support the development of statistical intuition

Players shoot at descending aliens in the style of old arcade games. The aliens fall according to a horizontal statistical distribution (e.g., they are more likely to descend in some locations than in others). To end a round, players have to set a bomb tuned to the frequency of the "mother ship" by picking which of the shapes on the right side best describes the shape of the ship dropping the aliens. The goal is to help students develop intuitions about patterns within chance.

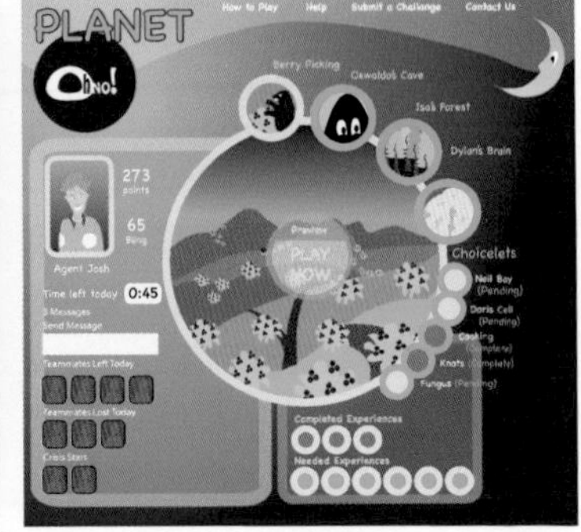

Plate 4 (Figure 10.1)

A platform for crowdsourcing the design of assessments

The left side shows the children's portal into the environment. The right side portrays the main interface where students can access various (assessment) games, accumulate points, and so forth. Through "kidsourcing," students play the assessment games, so it is possible to refine them. The bottom of the figure depicts some of the graphic assets available to anyone who wants to design choice-based assessments in *Planet Ohno!*

5 Preparation for Future Learning

A second major problem with knowledge, in addition to its isolation, is that a knowledge assessment is a description of a purportedly stable mental state. Assessment designers try to ensure that they are detecting a stable state and not a temporary effect, for example, by doing test-retest reliability measures. Knowledge is taken as an end or start state; it is not about learning per se. This concern with capturing knowledge states rather than dynamic change has had major implications for assessment. The first has been an emphasis on problem solving. The second has been a focus on mastery. While both are good, they do not directly emphasize learning, and they miss experiences that prepare people to learn. We detail these points next, while describing an alternative type of assessment that looks at learning itself.

Problem Solving without Learning

The cognitive revolution has stressed problem solving and, unfortunately, largely left the learning emphasis of behaviorism behind. (Whatever one might think of the restricted explanations of behaviorism, its focus on the tight connection between learning and motivation was a great strength.) A perusal of the finest cognitive psychology textbooks (e.g., Anderson 2000) reveals scores of constructs that explain the knowledge organizations and processes that affect problem solving—schemata, priming, working memory, echoic buffers, attention shifting, and so on—but only a handful of constructs to explain learning, most of which emphasize memory encoding and retrieval (e.g., association and consolidation). Attempts to make knowledge more dynamic by using the active verb *knowing,* or *knowing in action,* suffer the same problems: they are about problem solving and not learning.

Users of knowledge assessments can *infer* learning by giving the same assessment as a pretest and posttest. This is quite rare in educational practice; few teachers give pretests to measure subsequent learning gains, in part because it detracts from instructional time. Even if they did, wouldn't it be more to the point to evaluate learning directly?

Bransford and Schwartz (1999) labeled most current assessments as *sequestered problem solving* (SPS). In the typical SPS assessment, students are sequestered (like a jury) from learning opportunities and outside resources that might contaminate the validity of the assessment. Learning during a test would be cheating. Consider the following informal example of the shortcomings of SPS assessment.

A late-night talk show host asks a group of students who have just graduated from Harvard a handful of tricky questions like, "Is the earth closer to the sun in June or December?" or, "What is the best way to reintroduce a baby eagle to the wild?"

To the delight of the audience, the Harvard grads fare no better on these questions than a group of high schoolers. This assessment purports to demonstrate that the experience of going to Harvard does not produce the learning gains one would expect. The television show *Are You Smarter Than a 5th Grader?* has capitalized on making otherwise-educated people look stupid. Adults often do not recall the facts that the show asks, and the fifth graders regularly do. Other examples include the frequent polls that indicate that Americans do not know basic facts that must have been covered in school or newspapers.

What these scenarios actually demonstrate is that SPS assessments do not tell the whole story, though they do capture the public mind for what it means to have learned. Imagine, instead, what would happen if both groups of students were given access to learning resources during their quizzes. The Harvard students would probably use the learning opportunity to produce responses that outshone those of the high schoolers. Similarly, the adults would probably be better at finding the answers to the questions than the fifth graders (although one never knows how they choose the adults to be on such a program).

Here is a second, simple thought experiment. Imagine that a firm wants to hire a financial analyst. Tom has just completed a two-week course in Excel—his first exposure to spreadsheet software. Sig has not learned Excel. Instead, using multiple spreadsheet packages over the past several years, he taught himself, achieving high levels of expertise. The company decides whom to hire by using a paper-and-pencil test of basic Excel operations that just happen to have been covered in Tom's course. Tom would probably do better on this SPS test. We suspect, however, that Sig would be more likely to serve the company well in the long run. His deeper understanding of spreadsheet structure and capacity to learn independently will enable him to learn and adapt on the job—for example, when the company switches to a new software package or when the employees are asked to learn advanced features of Excel on their own. The failure of SPS tests is one reason that all employers would prefer to hire people for a trial period to see if the employee adapts to and learns in their local context. Edwin Ghiselli (1966) reported that aptitude tests only predict 9 percent of job performance immediately after training, and subsequently drop to 5 percent after time on the job. This is because people learn on the job, and sequestered assessments like aptitude tests are not designed to predict people's future learning.

An alternative to a static SPS assessment is a *dynamic assessment.* Reuven Feuerstein (1979) introduced dynamic assessments as an alternative to the standard administration of IQ tests. During the test, he would assist children, and therefore would see if they could learn from his help to solve the IQ problems. By using a dynamic assessment, he was able to make more useful diagnoses about children's learning potential.

Bransford and Schwartz (1999), who were concerned that theories of transfer were only focusing on the application of knowledge rather than learning, proposed a dynamic assessment format they termed *preparation for future learning* (PFL). In a PFL assessment, there are resources for learning during the test, and the question is whether students learn from them. Bransford and Schwartz reasoned that PFL assessments would be sensitive to differences in instruction that would be missed by static SPS tests. As support, Schwartz and Taylor Martin (2004) contrasted SPS with PFL assessments in the context of teaching statistics to ninth-grade students. In this experiment, one factor was how students were taught. Half the students received direct instruction, and the other half completed a form of guided discovery called "inventing" (cf. Schwartz, Chase, Oppezzo, and Chin 2011). A week later the students completed a long test. At the end of the test, there was a problem beyond the edge of what they had been taught.

The experiment crossed the instructional factor with a second one that involved the test itself. For half the children in each instructional condition, the tests simply included the difficult target problem without any resources for learning during the test. Thus, the students who used this form of the test completed an SPS assessment. The other half the students in each instructional condition completed a PFL version of the test. In the middle of the test, there was a worked example that students had to follow to solve an accompanying problem. The worked example showed how to solve a new kind of statistics problem, and students had to follow the worked example to solve a similar problem on the exact same page. All the students did well at copying the worked example to solve the associated problem. The main question, though, was whether the students would learn from the worked example. Unbeknownst to the students, the information in the worked example part of the test held the key to solving the hard problem at the end of the test.

Figure 5.1 shows the main results for how well students performed on the difficult problem at the end of the test. First,

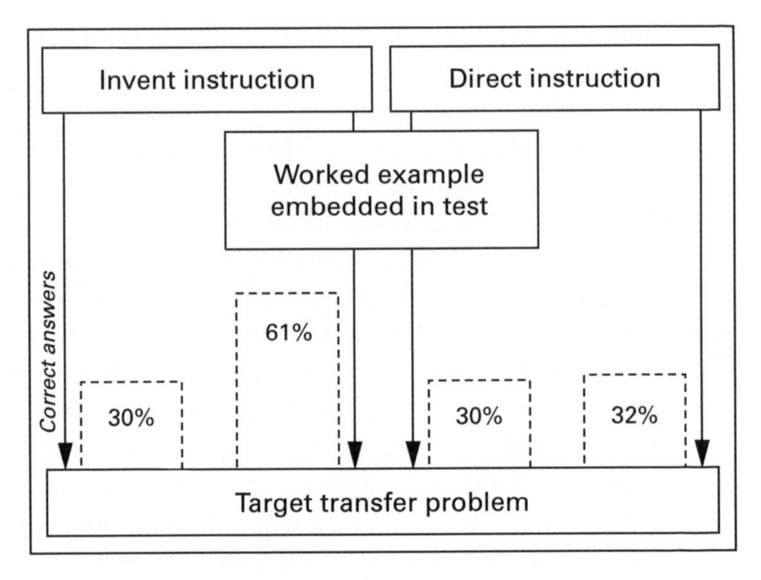

Figure 5.1
Improving the assessment of instruction by evaluating students' abilities to learn during a test
The students represented by the arrows in the middle of the graph received a learning resource as part of their test. This "learning during the test" assessment made it possible to differentiate the value of the two forms of instruction shown in the upper boxes. The students who did not receive the learning resource (the outer arrows) performed the same, which would have erroneously led to the conclusion that the two instructional treatments had the same value. (Adapted from Schwartz and Martin 2004.)

notice the levels of performance on the far right and far left of the graph. These are the levels of performance of the students who received the SPS version of the test, which did not include the worked example resource. By this SPS assessment, both forms of instruction led to the same outcomes, and one might naturally conclude that there is no advantage for one type of instruction over the other. Next, look at the two center bars indicating how well students did on the PFL version of the assessment. These are the students who received the worked example in the middle of their test. In this case, the invent instruction students doubled the performance of the direct instruction students. The invent instruction had better prepared students to learn during the assessment and then spontaneously use this learning. The simple point of this extended research example is that the use of dynamic assessments that include opportunities for learning can tell us a good deal more about the effects of instruction than can tests that simply measure static knowledge.

Mastery without Change

Knowledge provides a poor account of change. Either one has it or one does not, and knowledge-based accounts have trouble explaining how knowledge bootstraps itself from one state to another. This was highlighted in the learning paradox offered by Plato (*Meno*, 80.d):

> But how will you look for something when you don't in the least know what it is? How on earth are you going to set up something you don't know as the object of your search? To put it another way, even if you

come right up against it, how will you know that what you have found is the thing you didn't know?

Knowledge-based theories cannot easily give an account of where fundamentally new knowledge comes from. This is one reason that people argue that certain human abilities are innate; they cannot explain how the abilities could have been learned (Chomsky 1966; Pinker 1994). It is also one reason why it has been so difficult to produce a satisfactory knowledge-based account of conceptual change. Where can new concepts come from, if they do not come from ideas one already has? But if they come from prior concepts, then they must not be new concepts. Such is the knot of knowledge-based accounts.

In assessment, the description of knowledge as a state has led to an emphasis on mastery. Tests emphasize the mastery of skills and knowledge: Do students have the state of knowledge or not? If they exhibit mastery, they have knowledge. If they do not exhibit mastery, they do not have knowledge.

How does a mastery emphasis interact with the goal of seeing whether students are prepared for future learning? One assumption appears to be that if we want to assess someone's preparation for future learning, we should see if they have mastered the past. This seems like the rationale behind the Scholastic Assessment Test (SAT). The test tries to predict college success by seeing if students have mastered the mathematics, reading, and writing from earlier lessons.

The idea of looking at prior mastery to predict future learning is reasonable, but there is a catch. Tests of mastery presuppose knowledge in a mature form, implying that anything short of mastery does not count as knowledge and cannot be assessed.

Yet this is not true. First, people have earlier forms of understanding that do not comprise full-blown, declarative or procedural knowledge but that are nevertheless crucial for future learning. Michael Polyani (1966) referred to this as tacit knowledge. Harry Broudy (1977) described it as *knowing with*, as distinguished from *knowing that* and *knowing how*. Second, it is possible to assess these earlier forms of understanding, if we create assessments that allow learning during the test.

The late Russian psychologist Lev Vygotsky ([1934] 1987, 200) neatly captured the peril of mastery assessments:

> Like a gardener who in appraising species for yield would proceed incorrectly if he considered only the ripe fruit in the orchard and did not know how to evaluate the condition of the trees that had not yet produced mature fruit, the psychologist who is limited to ascertaining what has matured, leaving what is maturing aside, will never be able to obtain any kind of true and complete representation of the internal state of the whole development.

Knowledge-based assessments that can only detect mature forms of knowledge miss many of the important precursors of learning. One of PFL assessments' key benefits is that they can detect immature forms of understanding that SPS assessments miss. This makes them well suited to studying the types of informal learning that are so prevalent in today's information-rich ecosystem, because these types of learning often yield significant experiences that cannot be detected by mastery-focused tests.

For example, PFL assessments can be useful for evaluating digital game-based learning. James Paul Gee delivered a keynote to game researchers at the 2010 International Conference on the Foundations of Digital Games in which he mentioned that games could and should be used as preparation for future learning. It is easy to imagine how digital games might serve in this role. The rich experiences offered by gameplay are likely to produce tacit knowledge that is not easily measured by SPS tests of knowledge but that might be detected by PFL assessments. Players of the popular video game *Portal*, for instance, have ample opportunity to experiment with conservation of momentum, yet lacking some formal explanation of the phenomenon, the players would probably not do well on a physics test given in an SPS format. A PFL physics test, however, could provide a link between the players' experiences in the game and the formal physics concepts, thereby revealing the advantages for those who played *Portal* compared to a control group that did not play the game before taking the test.

To test the idea that the experience provided by digital games could serve as preparation for future learning, we built a game designed to help students learn the basic concepts of probability distributions (Arena and Schwartz 2010). Statistics is a notoriously difficult topic for people to learn and reason about (Nisbett, Krantz, Jepson, and Kunda 1983). One reason is that people naturally reason about single outcomes rather than distributions of outcomes. For instance, they often believe that the goal of statistics is to predict a single outcome versus a pattern of outcomes (Konold 1989). Making a "point prediction" reflects a causal form of reasoning as opposed to a statistical one. To the novice, random often connotes "without pattern," so the idea of statistics, where randomness supports inferences, can be difficult to grasp. We believed that one way to address this problem was to provide students with experiences that would give them intuitions about patterns of randomness (i.e., distributions) and probability before they received explicit instruction. Thus, our goal was not to produce a game that would teach students everything they needed to know about probability distributions (a bleak prospect for a game). We instead wanted to produce a game that would give students experience interacting with and thinking about probability distributions informally, so that when they received a subsequent exposition about probability, their gameplay experiences would help them understand the formal concepts. To that end, our game makes no explicit references to probability terms or concepts.

Figure 5.2 (plate 3) shows that in the game *Stats Invaders*, players simply shoot aliens dropping from the sky while trying to determine which of two displayed patterns (actually probability distribution curves) best describes the pattern in which the aliens are dropping. Once students have made their determination, they pick one of the two distributions on the right. This launches a bomb that is tuned to explode a mother ship in the same distribution (the game is a bit "male"). If the player picks the right bomb, the mother ship hidden above the descending aliens is destroyed. If not, the player loses a life—one of the standard tricks of video games.

In a study of the effectiveness of the game, we adapted the same research logic from before, where we compared SPS versus PFL measures of learning. As a pretest, a group of community college students completed a brief questionnaire about randomness and probability distributions with questions like, "What is the purpose of finding the pattern for a type of random event?" and, "What is the defining characteristic of a uniform distribu-

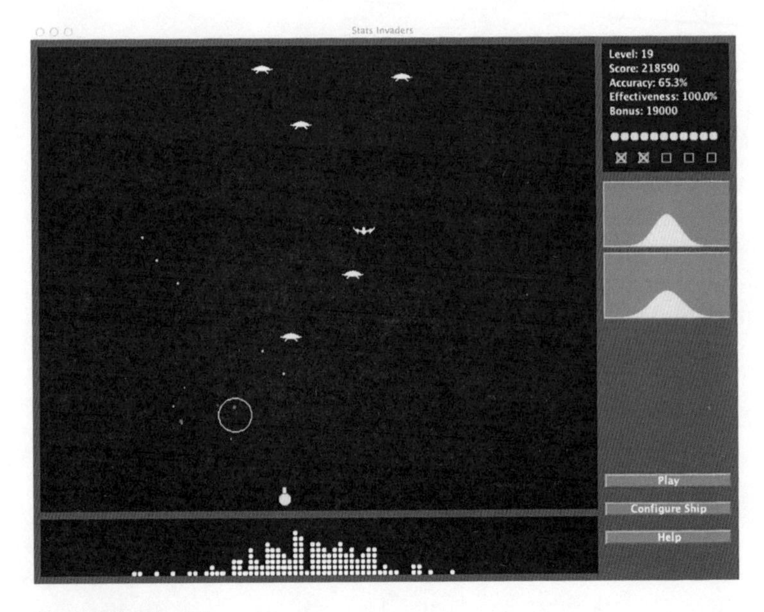

Figure 5.2 (Plate 3)

Stats Invaders: A video game to support the development of statistical intuition

Players shoot at descending aliens in the style of old arcade games. The aliens fall according to a horizontal statistical distribution (e.g., they are more likely to descend in some locations than in others). To end a round, players have to set a bomb tuned to the frequency of the "mother ship" by picking which of the shapes on the right side best describes the shape of the ship dropping the aliens. The goal is to help students develop intuitions about patterns within chance.

tion?" Then we had half the students play our game and half not. Next, half the students in each condition received a short reading passage on patterns in randomness. Finally, we gave all the students another test just like the first one. There were two key questions. Would playing the game improve performance on the test in its own right? And more important, would students who had played the game learn more from the passage than those who had not played the game?

Figure 5.3 shows gains from the first test to the second. Students from both groups learned from the passage, but students in the gameplay condition learned much more than students in the no-gameplay condition. The game players were able to relate what they were reading to their recent experiences in the game. Playing the game developed the earlier forms of knowledge that prepared the students to learn when given a chance. The game had created a time for telling (Schwartz and Bransford 1998). Notably, if we had not given the students a chance to learn, this benefit of the game would have gone undetected. Assessments that involve learning as part of the test can diagnose the benefits of intuitively compelling experiences that are missed by static knowledge tests. In chapter 7, we provide an example of a different type of PFL assessment that we used to evaluate whether popular commercial video games prepare students for future learning.

In the two cases of PFL assessments for statistics learning, the PFL assessment ultimately depended on a knowledge posttest. Students received posttests that examined whether they could answer questions based on the knowledge that had been told to them. This was valuable because it helped to validate the PFL

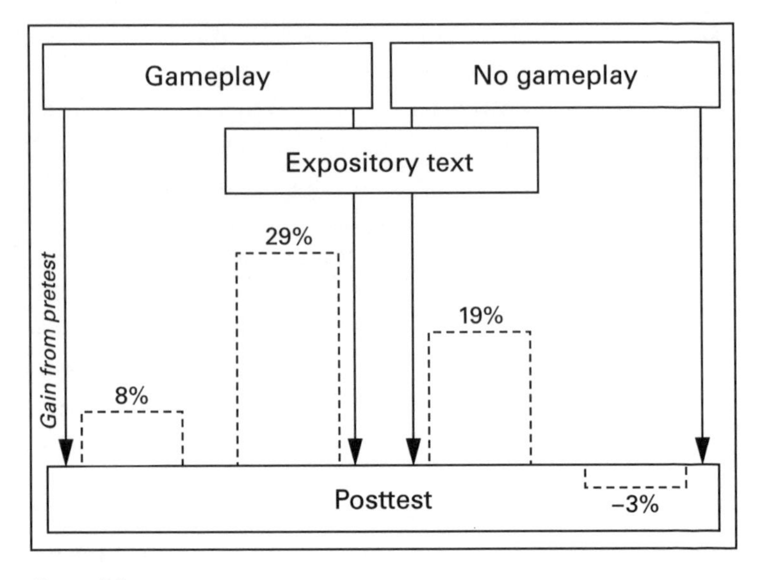

Figure 5.3
Benefits of gameplay in preparing students for future learning
Students who played a specially designed game to develop statistical intuitions learned more from an exposition on randomness than students who had not played the game.

approach to assessment using current standards and terms. One can only imagine trying to convince a policymaker about the value of new forms of assessments, if those assessments completely abandoned familiar terms. It would be like arguing that the gross domestic product (GDP) should be replaced by gross domestic happiness (GDH). Measuring happiness is not going to get very far in policy debates, despite the fact that it is closer to the goals of the citizens. To convince people that the GDH is a useful index, one would show that it supplies useful data that capture the value of the GDP measure, but that it also provides even more value. Therefore, our strategy is to first show that new forms of assessment offer added value, for example, by capturing what people think they care about in current terms (knowledge gains), while also capturing new information.

Our next task is to show that it is possible to use a choice-based approach to a PFL assessment. For example, Ryan Baker, Sujith Gowda, and Albert Corbett (2011) found that student choices of how to use help in an intelligent tutoring system predicted students' subsequent learning. The next chapter provides further relevant cases. After that, the final task is to show that choice-based assessments predict (and can change) future choices, thereby completely removing knowledge tests from the loop. We have not yet completed this final step (nor have we finished with the others). As neatly stated by José Ortega y Gasset (1960, 200), "Reason is not a train leaving at a fixed hour." We do not think people are ready to fully abandon knowledge until many people, including ourselves, help set forth strong evidence and reasons that we can do better.

III Practical Matters

6 Choice-Based Assessments of Learning

Thus far, we have made the argument that new technologies support new forms of interactive instruction and assessment that align with the normative mission of education. We have also contended that assessments organized around knowledge are too far removed from the realm of action and the future learner adaptations that education cares about, and that knowledge has inherent theoretical limitations for assessment. Our goal has been to convince people that there may be some value in considering a new interpretative framework for understanding learning and designing assessments.

Now, we turn to more practical matters. We show what happens when choice-based assessments are used in a PFL paradigm. Analyzing students' choices while they are learning provides information that goes beyond knowledge-based assessments. We begin with a simple experiment that directly compares choice- and knowledge-based assessments for their predictive value. The example uses a simple puzzle to make the demonstration. From there, we move to more substantive instances that reveal the effects of graduate school, the impacts of persistence in learning biology, and the development of basic mathematics in primary school children.

Head-to-head Comparison of Choice and Knowledge Assessments

Anna Rafferty (2007) directly compared choice- and knowledge-based assessments. The participants in her study worked with the interactive table shown in Figure 6.1. It is like a multiplication table except that the diamond represents a mystery operator that uses letters instead of digits.[1] To determine the function of the mystery operator, the participants guessed what belonged in each cell. They knew there was a lawful relation, and their task was to discover what it was. When the participants clicked on a cell to guess its entry, their click generated choice data (i.e., which cell they chose). They then used a pull-down menu to guess what letter belonged in the cell. This provided the data on their knowledge, with correct selections indicating higher knowledge. After completing this task, the participants received a transfer task, in which they had to learn and complete a new table that was governed by a different relation. The main research question of the study was which aspect of performance—knowledge or choice—on the first task better predicted successful learning on the second task.

To analyze the choice data, machine learning algorithms looked for instances in which the participants seemed to be trying to track down patterns. For example, if the participants clicked on several consecutive cells in the P column, these choices suggested that they were systematically uncovering the identity relation (P value in all cells of the column). On the other hand, if the participants clicked haphazardly from cell to cell, then their choices indicated that they were not on a productive path. The analysis of the knowledge data was simply how many correct answers the participants produced.

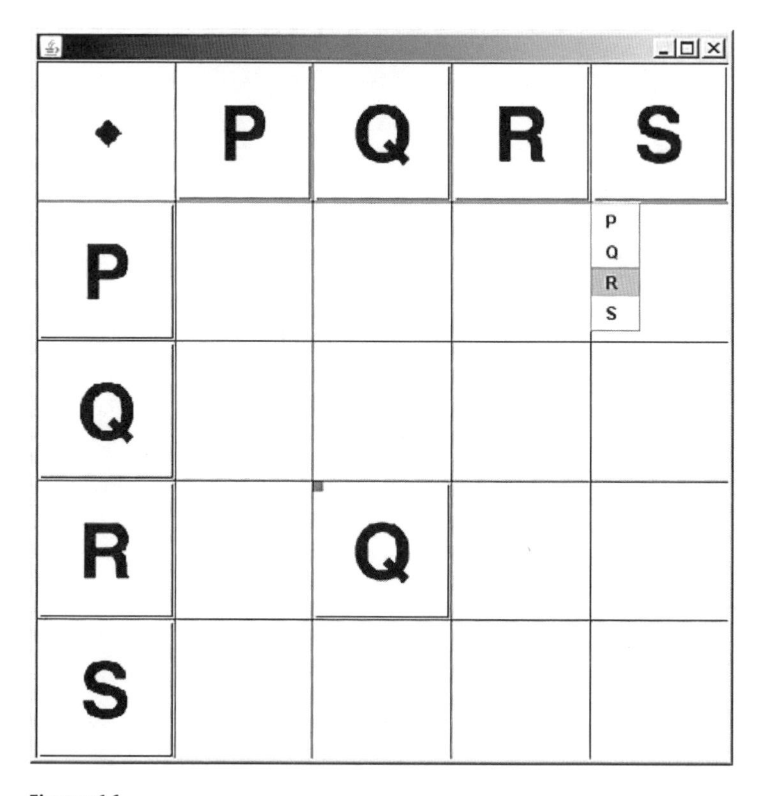

Figure 6.1

Task used to compare choice and knowledge assessments

Students tried to predict which letter showed up in each square. Their choices of which squares to test were more predictive of future learning than was the accuracy of the answers they gave for each square.

Both knowledge and choice separately predicted learning on the second task, but choice was a significantly better predictor. Moreover, in a second condition, the participants were not allowed to make choices about which cells to click. Instead, the system determined which cells they had to try. The participants in this case did worse on the transfer task. Thus, choice was better both as an assessment of how well the participants would learn in the future and it was better as a support for learning.

A more substantive demonstration of the value of a choice-based assessment comes from a study that compared graduate and undergraduate students. Knowledge-based assessments often tally up how well students solve a series of separate problems on a test. For instance, on an algebra test, one might find the percentage of correct answers across twenty problems. Given that the problems are presented as separate items, many students try to answer each problem separately. The same is true for many problems in textbooks, where each problem is usually viewed in isolation. But answering each question in isolation is not an optimal way to learn. A better way is to develop a general explanation or solution that can handle any relevant question (Schwartz, Chase, Oppezzo, and Chin, 2011). Lee Martin and Schwartz (2009) designed a choice-based assessment to see if they could detect the effects of graduate school on students' search for the general explanation.

Undergraduate and graduate students completed a diagnosis task that involved six fictitious diseases that each had multiple symptoms. Different diseases could share subsets of symptoms, which made it a hard diagnosis task. The students received twelve reference cases (patient files), each on a separate sheet of paper, to help them. Each sheet indicated the symptoms and diagnosis for one patient. The students had to use the reference cases to help diagnose ten new patients. The new patients were presented on a computer. For each new patient, the students ordered medical tests to reveal symptoms, and when ready, made their diagnosis. They received feedback on their diagnosis and moved on to the next patient.

The undergraduate students were drawn from the general Stanford University population, of which over half were pursuing a science- or engineering-related field. The graduate students were drawn from disciplines that involved complex information management (e.g., computer science, engineering, and biology), but none of them had completed diagnoses like these or had medical training.

Both the undergraduate and graduate students diagnosed the ten new patients with roughly 90 percent accuracy. The striking difference was that the undergraduate students were nearly done diagnosing the ten patients at about the same time that the graduate students began with their first patient. Evidently, graduate school teaches students to be slow.

What happened? All the graduate students spent a substantial portion of time working with the reference cases (patient files) before turning to diagnose the new patients. They made various representations such as matrices and decision trees. These representations created a compact depiction of the relations between symptoms and diseases, which became a "smart tool" or general solution for handling any possible case. Only after completing this representation did the graduate students begin diagnosing the new patients on the computer, and once they started their diagnoses, they never looked back to the original reference cases. In contrast, only 18 percent of the undergraduates bothered to make a general solution. They instead dove straight into the new patients. With each new patient, after they revealed a symptom, the undergraduates would shuffle through the reference cases to see what the symptom might mean.

Even though the undergraduate and graduate students were equally accurate, there was a hidden advantage for the graduate students. To evaluate each of the ten patients, it was necessary to order tests to find the absence or presence of specific symptoms. The graduate students were more "cost-effective" because they were able to diagnose each patient with fewer tests.

One probable explanation for these results is that graduate school provided many experiences handling data. Graduate school in empirical domains involves a good deal of trying to figure out one's own research data. When trying to explain data, one does not try to solve a single problem. Rather, one attempts to find a parsimonious explanation for all the patterns in the data. Perhaps these experiences led the graduate students to work toward a single general representation before testing it out on the ten new patients. In contrast, the undergraduates had learning experiences that emphasized the rhetorical task of getting the right answer using what they had been told in class. They focused on solving each problem in turn.

While these explanations are speculative, one explanation that does not work has to do with knowledge of the task, or knowledge of how to create a representation of the data. Other conditions in the experiment indicated that when pushed to make an organizing visual representation of the data, the undergraduate students were able to do so. Thus, the critical factor was whether the students chose to create a visual and general solution.

From our read of the literature, this is a rare demonstration of the effects of sustained inquiry, specifically graduate school, on how people subsequently go about learning something new (for another example, see Wineburg 1991 also discussed below).[2] It took an analysis of choices to find the effect. More generally, it is interesting to note that most assessments that attempt to measure the general effects of a college education often miss the point of a liberal arts education. They measure facts, skills, and problem solving (e.g., http://www.collegiatelearningassessment.org). But the point of liberal arts is to prepare students to continue learning throughout life by making wise learning choices.

Where Knowledge Cannot Tread

Knowledge-based assessments, because they focus on cold cognition, do not provide a good index into motivation. Choice-based assessments offer a way to generate behavioral data on motivational profiles. This is useful because it examines motivation in response to specific contextual conditions.

Catherine Chase (2011) recently tested a choicelet to measure an element of *intelligent persistence*. This choicelet was in the form of a game. It included five separate "planets," each targeting a different subtopic of genetic inheritance. On each planet, there was a brief challenge on the relevant subtopic. The challenges depended on topics in genetic inheritance that students had yet to learn, so it was a PFL assessment. Students had to learn while playing the planet game. To help them, students had access to resources for learning (e.g., readings and corrective feedback), and they received points for winning challenges. At any time, students could move to and from the planets as well as any of the learning resources, with their choices logged for later analysis. After finishing the game, students took a paper-and-pencil posttest on inheritance.

The key analysis involved what students chose to do after they lost a planet challenge: Did they stick with the planet and challenge, or did they leave the planet to play a different one? Also, did students' choices to persist or not provide any useful information? The rate at which students chose to leave a game room after failure was extremely diagnostic. As a simple correlation, leaving after failure explained 50 percent of the variance in how well students learned genetics from the game (as measured by the posttest). It also explained 33 percent of the variance in students' science classroom achievement (which in this case was eighth-grade physics, not biology). The measure of leaving after failure was more predictive of performance in the game and science class than were the frequency of game failure, pretest scores, standardized measures, and motivational surveys. Choice behavior can provide information missed by standard tests of knowledge, and choice behavior is more effective at predicting learning than are motivational surveys (a typical approach to noncognitive assessments).

As a final example, we return to the problem of assessing learning that precedes full-blown knowledge. We provided the example earlier of *Stats Invaders*, where students developed intuitions about statistics that we could detect with a separate PFL assessment. Here, we integrate the assessment into the learning environment. We show that analyzing choices can provide access to critical aspects of learning that precede full-blown knowledge, yet are regularly missed by mastery-oriented tests.

Most assessments focus on student knowledge by asking what schema, concept, or skill set must they have in mind. But if students have not mastered the relevant knowledge, it is difficult to make much headway beyond saying they do not have the knowledge. In the language of assessment, an item that students do not have the knowledge to answer yields little useful information about their ability levels. Examining choices offers more information.

Kristen Blair (2009) examined children's learning in a simulation environment intended to teach mathematical grouping. Figure 6.2 shows that students entered numerical values in the upper-right corner. A character named SpiderKid used these values to shoot webs different distances to rescue a cat. The figure depicts an advanced level in the game where students had to enter both the distance of each web (place value) and how many of them were needed (face value). The game reflected the recursive structure of numerical bases (e.g., the familiar base-ten, place-value system). The game was designed to create *implication feedback* (Blair 2009). Students could see the implications of their quantitative specifications because SpiderKid would go too far, not far enough, or to the right spot based on what the students had entered. This is different from simply saying that students are right or wrong, or just showing them the correct answer.

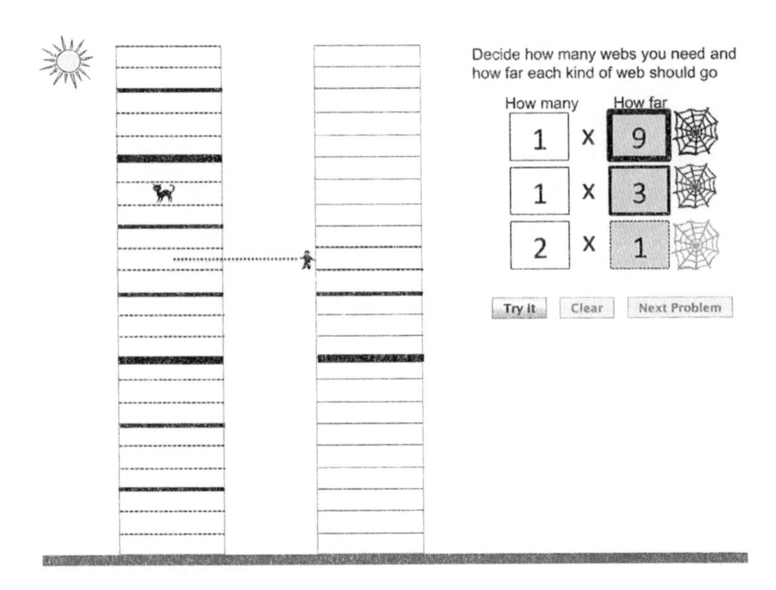

Figure 6.2
Screenshot of SpiderKid game
As part of a game to teach place value, children had to learn how to make the right-side ladder look like the left-side ladder so they could rescue a cat. The children entered values for the length of different colored webs and also how many of each web length to use (i.e., they entered place and face values).

Many children were not very good at the task early on. By analyzing the students' choices in response to feedback, Blair discovered that the children were failing because they did not perceive the feedback provided by the environment. They did not see the precise differences between the Spiderkid's climbing pattern on the left and the pattern of the building on the right. The problem was not what students were doing with the information in their heads; it was that the information never got in there in the first place. By looking at their choices, Blair identified a stable learning progression in the children's abilities to perceive increasing amounts of structure in the feedback: right/wrong information; too high or too low information; way too high/low or slightly too high/low information; and finally, the precise distance and direction of the discrepancy. Students who moved through the complete progression learned the matching recursive structure, whereas students who stalled at earlier levels never did.

In this example, analyzing learner choices supported assessments of what students could perceive and how this evolved, which is different from assessing what the students knew. If Blair had only assessed what students knew, the answer would have been "nothing" until the students finally solved the problems.

In this chapter, we provided four examples of choice-based assessments. In each case, the choices made by the participants supplied better insight into their learning than assessments of their knowledge. One goal of this chapter was to offer the existence proof that choice-based assessments can provide strong added value to the assessment enterprise. Of course, there are going to be instances where a poorly designed choice-based assessment does worse than a well-designed knowledge-based one. We do not want to make the claim that choice-based assessments are always better, though we do assert that choice-based assessments can measure a broader range of learning outcomes.

A second goal was to provide some sense of the range of phenomena that are within the measurement space of choice-based assessments that occur during learning. These include measures of strategy (tracking down mathematical patterns), measures of metacognition (seeking the general explanation), measures of persistence (trying to learn after failure), and measures of abilities to perceive (noticing the structure in feedback). This is quite different from just measuring right or wrong, and suggests the breadth of new kinds of things we might want to measure.

For instance, imagine that one wanted to measure the value of visiting a science museum. This is an elusive problem. First, it is difficult to get museum visitors to take a test. It seems possible, however, to give visitors an address to a Web site with follow-up games they could play and that are also choice-based assessments. This is likely to have more appeal than asking visitors to take a test. Second, and perhaps more difficult, any visit to a given museum exhibit is a short-lived experience for a visitor, so the effects would be subtle. The following is a thought experiment about how these subtle effects might be captured by an online, choice-based assessment.

One possible consequence of a museum experience is that it makes the content of the exhibits "sticky." The museum experience might create a small interest that helps future related information stick to that interest. The New York Hall of Science, for example, has an amazing exhibit on cosmic rays. It is a real-time physical exhibit that shows the presence of cosmic rays. A pool of cooled ethanol reveals the cosmic rays, because the rays create contrails in the liquid as they fly through (sort of like a bubble chamber in an atom smasher). If people put their hands over the pool, it does not block the cosmic rays—they pass right through the hands and leave undisturbed traces in the liquid. This seems like a sticky experience that could attune people to pick up more information about cosmic rays after they leave the museum.

To find out with a choice-based assessment, the visitors could receive a URL to play a game that has a lot of computer characters talking simultaneously, much like a party. At a select time, one of the characters among all the other voices could say a sentence that included the words "cosmic rays." Would the brains of the people who had gone to the exhibit "choose" to hear the sentence more than people who had not gone to the exhibit? (The analog is when people somehow hear their name at a party, even though all the other words in the crowd were just an unattended sound track until their name was spoken.) If people did hear the character say "cosmic rays," would they then choose to engage this character in the game? We certainly do not know the answer. What is more important is that we have a way to start finding out by using choice-based assessments of people's preparation for learning. There are many things we can measure given the ability to create and log new interactive contexts for learning.

7 Standards for Twenty-First-Century Learning Choices

In education, the decision about what to assess is largely driven by content standards. Standards create the possibility of accountability. The standards adopted by an educational system influence the textbooks written for that system, the daily instruction, and the assessments. Because of their importance, standards are often developed by high-powered committees. This can involve a good deal of negotiation about what is valuable for an educated citizen.

A concern with many standards is that negotiations yield laundry lists. An analogy comes from college English departments (and others, of course). All faculty members believe that their particular area of expertise should be considered mandatory for the students, whether or not it fits with everything else being offered. This produces something that is less coherent than one might want. It leads to the risk of a mile-wide, inch-deep curriculum.

Designers of assessments have to chase standards, coherent or not. If standards do not have a set of overarching principles, the designers of assessments also do not have a set of principles for translating the standards into assessments. This can lead to unhappy results. Consider the following 2011 California Standards Test for eleventh-grade U.S. history:

US11.1.2. Analyze the ideological origins of the American Revolution; the divinely-bestowed unalienable natural rights philosophy of the Founding Fathers and the debates surrounding the drafting and ratification of the Constitution; the addition of the Bill of Rights.

Now consider figure 7.1, which shows the assessment item designed to measure whether a student has achieved the standard.

While the example is extreme, it is not uncommon. A perfectly good content standard calling for the analysis of ideological debates has been dehydrated into a simplistic multiple-choice question about the name of the resolution. Busy teachers, recognizing that their students will be held accountable to the test, would be quite rational to skip the intent of the standard and teach the simple fact. Assessment designers (and teachers) need standards that provide overarching principles so they can decide whether a candidate assessment item fits the spirit of the standards. In the next paragraphs, we suggest two different types of frameworks. The first provides a high-level framework that may help prevent assessment choices that distort standards. It is also meant to clarify when it is important to assess choices instead of knowledge and skills. The second bridges between this high-level framework and the low level of actual assessment items by providing the ABCs of learning-oriented standards, where learning choices become part of the standards themselves.

A Framework for Highlighting When Choice-Based Assessments Are Most Relevant

A broader frame that stands above the standards can help facilitate local decisions about what should be taught and how

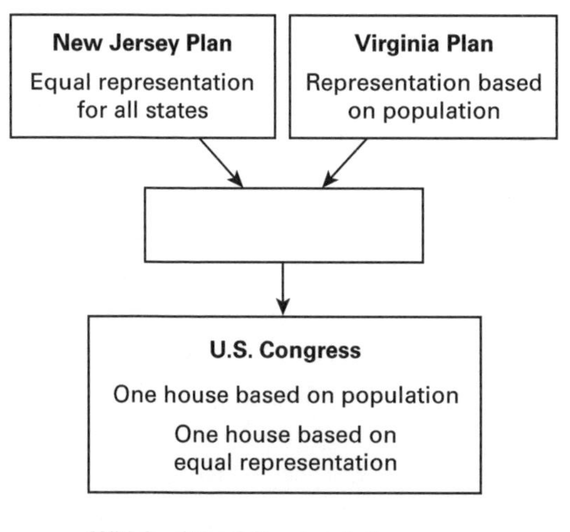

Which of the following belongs in the empty box above?

A The Missouri Compromise

B The Great Compromise

C *The Federalist Papers*

D The Articles of Confederation

Figure 7.1

A mismatch between standards and assessments

The assessment item is poorly designed to test the attainment of California Standard US11.1.2: "Analyze the ideological origins of the American Revolution; the divinely-bestowed unalienable natural rights philosophy of the Founding Fathers and the debates surrounding the drafting and ratification of the Constitution; the addition of the Bill of Rights."

it should be assessed (e.g., National Research Council 2012). One approach is to develop a model of what it means to be an educated person. Rather than a laundry list of competencies, the target of instruction and assessment would be more holistic. There is a common joke about developmental psychology textbooks: each chapter decomposes an aspect of child development to the point where there are no actual children in the textbook. It is an analog of the blind people each feeling a different part of an elephant and never being able to grasp the whole of the beast. A frame for standards could present a holistic model that helps keep in mind the recipients of education when designing for the many discrete competencies.

One solution embraced by cognitive science is to describe expertise (e.g., Ericsson 2009). A good model of expertise can assist people in backward engineering what the standards should include to achieve that expertise. For example, a portrayal of a chess master can help guide decisions about instruction and assessment for people trying to become chess masters. Using a model of expertise as a guiding framework can help prevent standards and assessments that are disjointed and do not cohere into a whole.

Giyoo Hatano and Kayoko Inagaki (1986) distinguished two types of expertise that are relevant to choice-based assessments: *routine expertise* and *adaptive expertise*. For recurrent situations of low variability, people can develop routine expertise: a set of rapid, consistent, and error-free routines. Hatano and his colleague Keiko Osawa (1983), for example, found that abacus masters could mentally add and subtract twelve-digit numbers presented two seconds apart, and had double the working memory for digits compared to the rest of the world. The abacus masters, through years of concerted practice, had developed an internal image of the abacus, which they used to track the quantities.

In the same study, Hatano and Osawa found that the astonishing skills of the abacus masters were highly specific and dependent on stable settings. The masters' working memory advantage was confined to digits—it disappeared for words and letters. Moreover, the abacus masters were intolerant of disruption, and they did not appear to use their skills to excel at other forms of mathematics. The abacus masters had developed expertise for a specific routine.

The dependence of these experts on routines led Hatano and his colleagues to propose adaptive expertise, which differs from the routine expertise of the abacus masters. Adaptive expertise is more appropriate for situations of high variability. Rather than replicating efficient routines, adaptive experts vary their behaviors and understanding in response to a changing environment. Hatano and Inagaki enumerated some of the characteristics of adaptive expertise that differentiate it from routine expertise: the ability to verbalize the principles underlying one's skills; the ability to judge conventional and unconventional versions of skills as appropriate; and the ability to modify or invent skills according to local constraints. Others have added to this list (e.g., deliberate practice, Ericsson, Krampe, and Tesch-Römer 1993; prospective adaptation, Martin and Schwartz 2009).

Schwartz, Bransford, and Sears (2005) built on Hatano's work to create the simple learning framework in figure 7.2. This framework distinguishes different outcomes of learning and

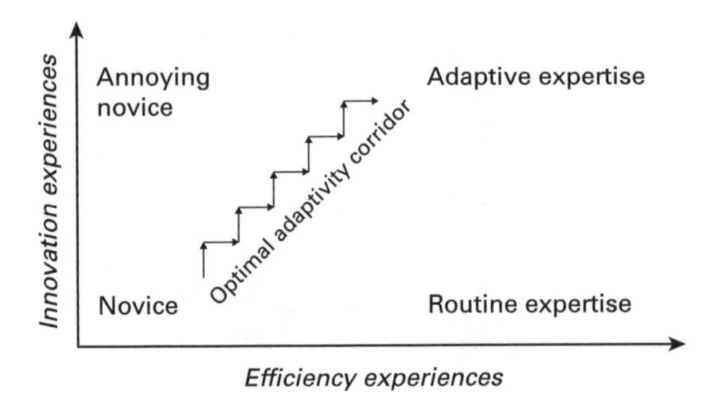

Figure 7.2
A broader learning framework for thinking about instruction, standards, and assessments (adapted from Schwartz, Bransford, and Sears 2005)

the trajectories that lead to them. The horizontal dimension emphasizes efficiency at specific tasks. Efficiency is especially important for recurrent situations, where it is better to rapidly and accurately remember as well as apply a solution, instead of figuring it out over and over again. The trajectory along this dimension leads to routine expertise, which comprises a set of efficient skills and retrieval patterns that are high on accuracy and speed with low variability in execution.

There are many topics in education that rightfully target routine expertise. The characteristic of those topics is that we can reasonably anticipate a stable performance environment in the future. In English, for instance, the letters are always read left to right, there is a space between words, and more generally, text appears in a stable format that permits a high degree of optimization. Good readers have developed such high efficiency for decoding words that it happens automatically on seeing a word, even when the readers try to avoid it (Stroop 1935). Highly efficient routines are important; struggles with decoding can interfere with reading for meaning (e.g., National Research Council 2007).

The vertical dimension in figure 7.2 stresses innovation experiences that involve handling novelty and variation. If students will have to adapt to a changing future, then they will need experiences that prepare them to invent new ways of understanding and doing things. Training the mastery of a given skill will not be sufficient. People need to be prepared to adapt—that is, learn something new.

A proposal embodied in figure 7.2 is that simply having students engage in innovative experiences is not sufficient to put them on a trajectory to adaptive expertise. Innovation without a strong body of understanding and efficient skills leads to inappropriate invention. Many readers have probably encountered "that guy" in meetings—the one who merrily brainstorms useless ideas and solutions, because he has no understanding of the constraints or topic. That guy is an annoying novice.

The optimal adaptability corridor (OAC) illustrates the goal of integrating experiences that support both efficiency and innovation. Many discussions in education pit these against each other—for example, discovery learning versus training (Tobias and Duffy 2009). This is a mistake, because there are different processes associated with efficiency and innovation, and therefore they do not displace one another. People need a balance of both. Adaptive experts are presumably high on both dimensions, with a strong set of efficient schemata and skills that they can adapt to handle new situations as well as challenges (e.g., Hatano and Inagaki 1986; Wineburg 1998).

The qualitative hypothesis of the OAC is that the balance of efficiency and innovation often works best when innovation experiences precede efficiency-oriented instruction that focuses on accuracy. If students learn the efficient solutions first, they will have little need to innovate and can miss what is novel (Schwartz, Chase, Oppezzo, and Chin 2011). But if they first attempt to innovate their own solution, they will develop a better appreciation of the relevant context and problem. This prepares them for future learning from formal expositions. When the efficient solutions are presented, students will appreciate why those solutions work so well.

Many undergraduate engineering and science programs spend the first 3.5 years teaching the efficient analytics (math), and then in the final semester students at last get to design or discover something. Using the framework in figure 7.2, students travel along the efficiency dimension for many years before they finally have innovation experiences. According to the OAC, it would be better to interleave efficiency- and innovation-oriented experiences. For instance, Jared Taylor, Karen Smith, Adrian van Stolk, and George Spiegelman (2010) found that compared to standard efficiency-oriented instruction, students who received a full course that involved inventing models in a college-level cell biology course (prior to receiving the relevant lectures) were more able to generate explanations for novel cell phenomena without any loss to their basic mastery of the course content. They were being better prepared for the explanatory work of real scientists.

For those skills and competencies that can reasonably anticipate a stable future and high repetition, the simplest and most appropriate assessment is to ask people to complete the task as fast as possible, with the fewest errors, with the least variability, and in a context as similar to the future performance context as possible. This would be the aforementioned approach of using SPS assessments, which measure movement along the horizontal dimension toward routine expertise and a high degree of mastery. Most knowledge and skills-based assessments take this form, and they are appropriate to the goal.

For competencies that cannot presuppose a stable future but instead will require adaptation, assessments should target the trajectory toward adaptive expertise. Choice-based assessments of students' preparation for future learning are appropriate. They examine the processes that students use to adapt, learn, and move along the diagonal.

As one example, a good assessment of student preparation for future learning asks students to choose what information they would like to receive so they can learn about a new topic (Bransford and Schwartz 1999). In a recent study (Arena 2012), community college students were randomly assigned to one of three conditions: a control condition in which they did nothing, a game condition in which they played fifteen hours of the commercial video game *Call of Duty 2*, and a game condition in which they played fifteen hours of the commercial video game *Civilization IV*. Both *Call of Duty* and *Civilization* are relevant to World War II.

On an immediate SPS posttest of their factual knowledge about World War II, the three conditions did not look different. By this measure, playing the video games had little value. The study also included two PFL assessments. The first took the familiar format from chapter 5. Students in the three conditions received a lecture on World War II to see if the games had prepared students for future learning. On the postlecture test, comprised of questions drawn from standardized tests, the game-playing students showed greater gains from the lecture. The PFL format of the test showed that students who had played the games were more prepared to learn about World War II, while the earlier SPS assessment missed these tacit effects of game playing. The second PFL assessment, which focused on the students' choice of questions, yielded a more precise description of their likely learning trajectory. Students from all three conditions were told historic battle scenarios from World War II. They were asked what questions they would like answered so they could understand what happened. Students who had played *Civilization* asked questions about the relationships among the nations in the scenarios (e.g., French and British), which makes sense because *Civilization* is a high-level strategy game. Students who had played *Call of Duty* asked questions about the local tactics of the battle, which also makes sense because *Call of Duty* is a first-person shooter game. Thus, the choice-based assessment that asked what students would like to know provided a good metric of the effects of their learning experiences and likely learning trajectory in the future.

The adaptive expertise framework is a high-level organization of major goals of instruction and therefore possible assessments. Hopefully it clarifies the province of knowledge-based assessments (routine expertise) versus choice-based ones (adaptive expertise) as well as the learning experiences that complement each.

The framework in figure 7.2 is a high-level abstraction. It is important to also have midlevel principles to close the gap between the abstract framework and nitty-gritty empiricism of assessment. This is the goal of the next section.

The ABCs of Twenty-First-Century Competencies

Adaptive expertise seems highly relevant to recent discussions about the skills and competencies needed for the twenty-first century. Proposals range from increased creativity to improved social skills as well as many others. The catalyst for generating lists of twenty-first-century skills comes from a realization that times have changed and will continue to do so. The lists are responsive to a vision of a future filled with rapid changes in work, communication, global interdependence, technology, and ideally learning. In this future, individuals' abilities to adapt to changes along with their abilities to innovate those rapid changes will largely be a function of their abilities to make effective learning choices.

The idea of twenty-first-century skills—twenty-first century or not—has captured the imagination of many. Lists of twenty-first-century skills often focus on innovation (the vertical dimension from figure 7.2), which has been lacking in many standards. These skills have not been well operationalized into assessments, however, in part because of the hegemony of knowledge-based assessments. Choice-based assessments suit the gist of twenty-first-century skills because they embody an inherently dynamic perspective that matches the realization that people will need to continue to learn and adapt.

The list of twenty-first-century skills and competencies needs to be actionable if it is meant to do more than sort students by their abilities. The skills have to be amenable to instruction and assessment. Oftentimes, there are confusions about which of the competencies can be taught. For example, many people propose that creativity is an innate personality trait rather than a learnable skill (e.g., Barron and Harrington 1981; Gough 1979). This is the wrong way to think about these competencies. The question instead is whether people choose to engage in them. In his review of creativity, Robert Sternberg (2006, 97) states, "Creativity is in large part a decision that anyone can make but that few people actually do make because they find the costs to be too high." From this perspective, people can learn to make the choice to be creative, assuming there are environments that support this choice.

If we were in charge of the world, which we are decidedly not, we would create a different type of list for twenty-first-century competencies. The list would emphasize ways of learning and adapting, and the choices to do so. We would call it the ABCs of learning choices to help people remember them. For each letter, there would be a description of a core mechanic for learning and the specific outcome of that mechanic. ("Core mechanic" is a term from game design. It refers to a game's driving interaction and its goal, such as shooting an enemy to stay alive.) Ideally, education would provide experiences in how and when to choose these different learning mechanics, plus what learning outcome one can reasonably anticipate. For example, making analogies is an excellent way to promote the transfer of learning from one topic to another, but it is a poor way to improve automaticity. Deliberate practice is a good way to improve automaticity, yet it is a poor way to improve transfer. Here are some ideas for the first few letters. In each case, there is a body of literature that describes how these work, what to do, and what to expect as a learning outcome. For simplicity, we just list the core learning mechanic:

- A is for Analogy
- B is for Brainstorming
- C is for Collaboration
- D is for Distinctiveness
- E is for Elaboration
- F is for Feedback
- G is for Generation
- H is for Hands-on
- I is for Interest

Of course, there are alternatives for each letter. For instance:

- A is for Associative Memory
- B is for Behavior Change
- C is for Contrasting Cases
- D is for Deliberate Practice
- E is for Explaining
- F is for Formalizing
- G is for Goal Setting
- H is for Helping
- I is for Inquiry

Debating which of these learning choices should be on the list of "twenty-first-century learning choices" strikes us as a productive exercise. The ABCs provide research-proven methods of learning that help people grow and adapt in specific ways. If fleshed out for specific topics and contexts (as we discuss below), the ABCs would make up a precise set of standards that would prepare students to become both efficient and adaptive. In this case, teaching to the test would entail teaching students how to learn for different desired outcomes.

It is important to avoid thinking that the ABCs are general learning skills that rise above specific domains of learning. There is a literature on "learning to learn" that refers to domain-general study skills (e.g., Olivier and Bolwer 1996). But few learning skills are truly domain general because they typically work better in some situation than others. For example, when learning to decode words, we want to emphasize learning techniques that improve automaticity. But when it comes to philosophy, automatic responses are probably a bad outcome.

A nice case in point comes from Sam Wineburg (1991) in his comparison of college students and professional historians. Working individually, they each received a set of source documents and had to explain what happened at the Battle of Lexington. The historians in the study were not experts in American history but they were trained in the routines of historical analysis. They did not assume that the words in each document were true; instead, they attempted to better understand the intent of the authors and the historical context in which the works were written. In contrast, college students did not attempt to explore and understand the perspective behind each data source; they tried to understand the documents based on their own experiences. The college students were using a general learning-to-learn strategy that they had gained over many years of schooling—namely, use current background knowledge to comprehend a text (Bransford and Johnson 1971; Anderson and Pearson 1984). It is a good strategy, but it does not apply to all learning domains, as in the case of interpreting historical documents. To understand the intent of an author from another era or culture, one often needs to learn new information about the social, cultural, and political conditions that existed when statements were made.

When it comes to learning as well as assessing learning choices, it is important to avoid the assumption of general skills and dispositions of learning that apply to any context. Using the preceding framework of adaptive expertise, an ideal assessment would look at students' choices as they learn specific content to see how well they are moving on a trajectory of adaptive expertise in that domain of endeavor.

Similarly, the ABCs should not be taught or assessed in decontextualized ways. Different types of learning strategies should be tied instead to contexts and practices where they are most appropriate. For example, we can make a matrix of the recent Common Core State Standards (http://www.corestandards.org), which present a national set of standards. At a rarified level, an assessment framework might look something like the following for an abbreviated subset of the standards for fourth-grade mathematics:

	Analogy	Brainstorming	Contrasting cases	Deliberate practice
1. Multidigit fluency				+
2. Fraction equivalence	+		+	
3. Classify 2-D shapes	+	+		

The noticeable aspect of the matrix is that learning mechanics have been integrated into the standards. Introducing learning mechanics into the standards encourages instruction on learning strategies, because the choice-based assessments would examine students' choices to use these types of learning mechanics. Tying learning mechanics to the content standards provides valuable guidance to assessment designers through stronger constraints on what is being measured.

Currently, standards include statements of what students should know or be able to do with their knowledge when they have finished learning. It is curious that standards include these loud directives regarding knowledge outcomes, but are silent about the means of learning. This exclusion may be a leftover from earlier times, when the science of learning had not matured as much as it has. Old (and not so old, but tired) debates about learning seem to pit one model against another, as though one size fits all topics and goals, and the big trick is to figure out just which size it is. Times have changed. One of the crucial discoveries of the past fifty years has been the realization of the many different systems that people have for learning and how they work for different domains of learning (e.g., implicit versus explicit learning; Schacter 1987). The learning sciences have revealed a great deal about the many different ways that people learn, and what each approach confers for different topics.

Developing a trajectory in any domain of endeavor requires several types of learning, ranging from skill acquisition to interest development to conceptual growth to domain-specific habits of mind. Key enablers of these trajectories are the participatory structures and range of resources available to learners (Ito et al. 2009). Unfortunately, most introductory college courses in science and mathematics serve a singular diet of lectures followed by problem sets followed by quizzes, midterms, and finals. This model of instruction, which is quickly becoming the new college textbook in video form (e.g., http://www.udacity.com), cannot achieve all the important learning goals of instruction. Rather, it feeds directly into knowledge-based assessments of facts and procedural fluency in problem solving. To create vibrant classrooms that engage as many students as possible, faculty should overcome the inertia of historical habits passed from generation to generation. Explicitly including different ways of learning as a component of standards (or any curricular definition) would go a long way in overcoming inertia and helping faculty and students develop a deeper understanding of how people learn. Grounding these standards in choice-based assessments would provide clear targets to help educators understand the goals of instruction.

IV Matters of Practice

8 The Tangle of Reliability and Reification

Many assessment questions are built on intuitions. For example, questions at the end of a chapter are often based on an author's sense of what would help students study more productively. Test banks that come with packaged curricula are frequently manufactured in odd ways, such as randomly sampling sentences from a textbook and then making one question per sampled sentence.

High-stakes assessments are another matter. The question formats may be similar to more intuitively developed tests (e.g., multiple-choice word problems), but there are stronger back-end methodologies for warranting that assessments measure what people think they are measuring. The stakes are higher, and the enterprise is much larger. The Educational Testing Service, with over twenty-five hundred employees, delivers fifty million tests per year.

The Educational Testing Service produces many creative products that measure all manner of human behavior. But the creativity and insight of these measures is not what gets communicated to the public or the average test maker. As Robert Mislevy, Linda Steinberg, and Russell Almond (2003, 2) put it, "Three decades of progress in fields that are central to assessment—cognitive psychology, measurement models, information technology, and learning in the disciplines—have had surprisingly little impact on everyday practice." People instead experience the same old test formats that were originally developed as simple solutions to formal problems in test development, such as reliability. In this section, we describe some of the unintended consequences that result from an assessment enterprise that has largely evolved to characterize individual differences and then sort learners with respect to these differences. We provide a brief tutorial on some technical practices of assessment development before moving forward to newer approaches in chapter 9 that we think can undo some of the unintended mischief done by current assessment methodologies. For example, rather than using assessments to sort students based on individual differences, it may work better to use them to sort the quality of learning experiences.

Constructs

Much of the formal work in human measurement revolves around *constructs*. A construct is "a product of informed scientific imagination, an idea developed to permit categorization and description of some directly observable behavior" (Crocker and Algina 1986, 230). Intelligence is an example of a construct. So is "knowledge that the earth is round" as well as "personal identification with science." None of these mental states can be directly observed in their totality, so they must be inferred from a sample of a person's behavior. One can see markers of intelligence, knowledge, and identification. But the construct is more than a single manifestation. The broader construct is the "product of informed scientific imagination." The imagination yields an argument that various observations cohere into something more fundamental that is responsible for producing a constellation of behaviors.

The Nobel physicist Leon Lederman (with Teresi 1993) provides a useful analogy for understanding the challenge of finding invisible constructs—in his case for subnuclear particles. He describes aliens (the Twilo) who come to earth and happen on a soccer match. They cannot see the colors black and white, which means they cannot see the soccer ball. They can see the players running, the goalie falling to the ground, and the crowd cheering. Their task is to figure out what organizes all these behaviors—that is, they need to infer the existence of a ball. It takes an inspired leap to posit an invisible construct. Moreover, once one posits the construct, it is necessary to decide which evidence is relevant and could confirm or falsify the existence of the construct.

The task of test makers is not that different. A person, researcher, or group of people may propose a construct such as "scientific identification." Because it is a new idea, the purported properties of the construct are poorly understood; it is not clear who has it or how much; and the measures that would reveal its existence are also unknown. It is a hard endeavor. The construct of intelligence provides an excellent example. Everybody has some intuitive sense that they can tell when they are talking to someone smart. Yet after years and years of test development and theorizing, there is no consensus on whether there is one intelligence construct or many. Nobody really knows what IQ tests measure other than performance on a test that is labeled "intelligence quotient." Even so, the IQ test has captured the beliefs of so many. The test (or any of its many modern variants) has *become* the construct of intelligence in the public mind, despite the fact that there is no scientific consensus on the construct itself. Here, we begin to see the reifying power of tests.

Validity

We can separate two criteria for a useful assessment: *validity* and *reliability*. All assessments are beholden to them. Validity and reliability are concepts for ensuring that the chain of reasoning from test scores to constructs is as strong as possible.

Validity is roughly analogous to accuracy. It refers to the extent to which scores on a test are actually related to the construct under investigation. A geography test that measures the time it takes each student to run a hundred yards might reliably sort the students into roughly the same order each time it is given, but it would not be a valid test of geography knowledge.

A good assessment reveals behavioral patterns that are valid warrants for the presence, absence, or strength of a particular construct in an individual. Mislevy, Steinberg, and Almond (2003) have developed a framework called evidence-centered design to help the designers of assessments navigate these complex waters. Evidence-centered design is a framework for developing and using tests that embrace the notion of assessment as an argument, or part of a chain of claims, supporting the characterization of a construct in a person. It includes various stages, but the core logic involves machinery to link up the following five components: a *student model* representing the constructs of interest, *evidence models* representing the relationships between those constructs and various behaviors, *task models* representing discrete tasks intended to serve as instances of the behaviors in the evidence models, an *assembly model* describing how to combine tasks appropriately to form a coherent assessment (an assessment is typically a combination of measures), and a *presentation model* describing how the assessment is presented to and completed by test takers. Evidence-centered design helpfully unpacks an argument logic that is familiar to experimental psychologists but may be foreign to assessment designers.

Reliability

There have been great advances in the field of psychometrics, yet there is a problem sitting in the middle of it all. It involves the concept of reliability. Reliability has a technical meaning, but basically it can be thought of as analogous to precision. It refers to the extent to which scores on a test remain consistent over time within a sample as well as the extent to which the items that make up the test all seem to be measuring the same thing ("hanging together" or "pointing in the same direction"). The basic statistic is an association (i.e., correlation). If people are high on one test item, are they high on all the other items from that test that claim to measure the same construct? If so, the test hangs together, and the warrant that there is a construct behind the performances on all the items is increased.

To see if the assessment is stable, a simple solution is to show that a person performs similarly on a test over several administrations. Unlike a yardstick, which has the property of length, a behavioral test does not *have* the property of interest. An IQ test is not smart. To ensure that a test is a stable index of a property, the test has to be taken. It has to be taken repeatedly, ideally by the same person, to ensure it gives the same measure. This way, one can rest assured that the assessment is immune to error introduced by the time of day, the mood of the test taker, or a host of other variables that mean the test is picking up some qualities not associated with the construct. If evaluators are trying to get a good fix on a person, they want to be sure that their measures do not exhibit slippage. If a person could show that the SAT gave different results at different times, and a university relied on SAT scores for admissions, one can imagine the legal battles. No one wants to use a yardstick that keeps changing its size from measure to measure.

Reliability is important. Through an unlucky coincidence (or maybe not a coincidence), however, the methodological demand of reliability coincides with a tendency of people to take an essentialist perspective that reifies assessments into stable traits or essences of a person—individual properties that do not change. Ray McDermott (1993) ironically describes how disability constructs "acquire" children, which in turn defines the children going forward, both inwardly and outwardly. Reified individual properties can range from disabilities to mastered knowledge to personality types to intelligence.

The combination of the need for a stable assessment and the simplicity of thinking in terms of stable traits can yield useful scientific advances. For example, a good deal of personality research focuses on the "Big Five" personality traits: openness, conscientiousness, extraversion, agreeableness, and neuroticism (Costa and McCrae 1992). There is even research that shows a correlation between the volume of specific brain regions and different personality types (DeYoung et al. 2010). But knowing that people have/are/derive from these five traits does not do much for improving learning. The assumption is that these five are stable personality traits, and therefore, the trait constructs seem misaligned with the goal of designing instruction to change them.

One unsuccessful way to use traits to improve learning is to assume that different types of people require different types of instruction. If someone is a "spatial thinker," for example, then they should receive "spatial instruction." Alas, this belief does not correspond well to current evidence when considering nonclinical populations. A contemporary form of the belief comes in the guise of *learning styles*: different people have different ways they learn best, as though a learning style were a fixed trait. The problem is that there is minimal evidence that shows that learning styles is a useful idea (Massa and Mayer 2006). Despite its capture of the public mind, to our knowledge nobody has convincingly shown the key attribute-treatment interaction. Such an interaction would show that some stable attribute, trait, or essence of the learner determines which type of treatment or instruction is the most effective. For instance, nobody has found that a "spatial" person learns better from spatial material than verbal material, or vice versa. The closest example that we know of has been the demonstration that low-IQ students benefit from well-organized material, whereas high-IQ students benefit from less-organized material (Snow

1989). (The high-IQ students work harder to untangle the less-organized material, which leads to deeper processing.) We can only imagine explaining to parents that it is better to confuse instruction for smart kids, rather than just giving the smart kids advanced materials that are well organized. In general, good instruction works for most everyone who does not have clinical-level difficulties.

The fact that some constructs, such as personality or intelligence, claim high reliability has unintended consequences on learning. Carol Dweck and her colleagues (Blackwell, Trzesniewski, and Dweck 2007) have documented that a good portion of the school population has reified the construct of intelligence. These people believe their intelligence is a fixed essence. When they fail at a task, they think that they are not smart enough and cannot change. As a result, they do not persist and do not learn. They are thinking, "What's the use of trying?" Intelligence is an unproductive construct when it comes to choosing to learn. Like other trait ascriptions, intelligence does not help people appreciate contextual supports and hindrances to their development (cf. Barab and Plucker 2002). And of course, the issue of assigning traits is not limited to intelligence and personality. The same problem shows up in knowledge domains, as when someone says, "I'm not a math person."

Interestingly, Dweck has found a way to ameliorate the effects with her Brainology program (http://www.mindsetworks.com/brainology). She helps children understand that their brains can change, for example, by explaining how neurons grow and connect. As a result, students exhibit more mastery behaviors, where they try to understand rather than give up. An interesting aspect of this solution is that it switches the narrative of learning. Rather than being about an essentialist construct of intelligence based on reliable IQ tests and reified abilities, this biological model provides an alternative interpretative framework for learning, much like we are trying to do with choice.

Education is about change through learning, yet our assessments need to demonstrate stable constructs. How can we solve this paradox? As we argued in chapter 5, one solution is to assess the dynamic process of learning per se as opposed to a static, easily ossified construct like knowledge. The next chapter describes two complementary alternatives.

9 New Approaches to Assessment Design

Sorting Experiences and Not Only Students

Current assessments are like rainwater on a roof, looking for a leak. Wherever there is a crack, they find a way to seep into people's beliefs about themselves. Changing the fundamental goal of assessments may help everyone stay a little drier. Most assessments are designed to sort students, which leads to personal attributions based on the test. Students can be sorted from best to worst (norm-referenced tests), or they can be sorted above or below some criterion of performance (criterion-referenced tests). We can change this function of assessments, though.

Rather than primarily designing assessments to sort learners, we can design them to sort learning experiences. In this application, the primary goal of the assessment is to draw an inference about the quality of a learning situation, and a secondary goal can be for drawing an inference about a child. This reverses the usual prioritization of assessment design, and could alleviate the natural tendency to identify people by virtue of a test.

Sorting situations is a well-known strategy for researchers who want to compare different forms of instruction. They might run an experiment where they implement two different types of instruction. Ideally, they have a strong situational construct that differentiates the two instructional treatments (e.g., the presence or absence of hands-on materials). They then look at student performances on a posttest. The goal is to make an inference toward the nature of instruction instead of any individual child. One of the appeals of this approach is that it yields actionable information about how to change the learning situation. So rather than thinking of how multiple items converge into a description of a child (e.g., from a ninety-minute survey with a mind-numbing proliferation of repetitive questions), the thought is how multiple students converge into a description of instruction using relatively few test items.

The important distinction here is whether an assessment is primarily intended to compare test takers—say, to sort students into advanced and remedial courses of math instruction—or experiences—to determine whether a new way of teaching math produces greater learning gains than standard practice. (It is key to note that because of the higher stakes involved, tests used in evaluations of individual test takers are rightfully subjected to greater scrutiny than are tests used in evaluations of experiences.) In the context of our discussion of choice-based assessment, we are primarily concerned with the latter type of test. We are more interested in discovering which features and arrangements of learning environments contribute to learning than we are in characterizing individual differences in learning proficiency. In our experience, knowing how to teach has a stronger effect than knowing which child has done poorly on a test. If we do not know what constitutes effective instruction, then knowing that a child has not learned does not get us very far.

Currently, assessments are predicated on person-level constructs. We do not fully understand why this is the case, though some of it has to do with the rise of individual differences research in psychology and the public belief about what is important to study. The certification of individuals is also a crucial function of assessments. A driving test certifies an individual as a capable driver who knows the rules of the road. Without a certification process, there would be more accidents (although clearly, our driving assessments are not perfect, which is one reason California does not permit unchaperoned teenagers to drive with other teenagers in the car). But if certification and stratification are their only functions, assessments designed to sort people instead of learning experiences miss the formative goals of assessments (Black and Williams 1998). Feedback from assessments should inform the design of and practices within the learning environment so learners can do better (e.g., Anderson, Zuiker, Taasoobshirazi, and Hickey 2011).

Many assessment efforts do attempt to provide feedback for evaluating the quality of learning experiences. For example, the PISA, an international test, is used to sort how well nations are educating their children. State-mandated tests are often used to evaluate how well different schools are functioning. In California, we receive children's performances on standardized tests, and the newspaper reports the overall performance of the school. Unfortunately, these reports are based on individual knowledge constructs, of which students have varying quantities.

Current assessment constructs locate knowledge in the head, and therefore one cannot locate the constructs in the environment. For instance, if students in school A do not know that 2 + 2 = 4, how do we locate the equivalent "knowledge" construct at the classroom level? Would we see what words or mathematical symbols the teacher or textbook is using? This does not constitute knowledge. Words are not knowledge. Words don't know anything. Given a finding that children at a school do not know basic math facts, one cannot infer much about the classroom learning experiences. Maybe the classrooms have lots of math words, but the instruction using those words is poor. Ideally, there would be assessments of learners that support stronger inferences about the nature of their learning experiences.

The mission of the Common Core Standards states that its goal is to "provide a consistent, clear understanding of what students are expected to learn, so teachers and parents know what they need to do help them" (http://www.corestandards.org). We suspect that most of the assessments that will be associated with these standards will not permit the desired bridge between standards and action. Knowledge-based assessments do not solve the problem of guiding teachers and parents to figure out "what they need to do." The constructs are largely about knowledge; they are not constructs one can use to describe a learning experience.

A simple solution is to use "process-oriented" constructs rather than knowledge-based ones. Making the constructs about processes of learning as captured through learning choices would enable a more direct translation between individual and classroom processes of learning. One could observe the processes of learning used in class and map them to the processes of learning that an individual uses to learn on the test, and vice versa. For example, we might observe the use of inquiry in a science classroom. We can also make choice-based assessments of individual's choices to use inquiry to learn. The construct of using inquiry to learn would span both the classroom and individual level. If the students from a given school or classroom did not use inquiry to learn in an individual assessment, it seems likely that one could look at their learning experiences and then find that those experiences also do not include sufficient opportunities and supports to use inquiry to learn. An assessment of individuals could help us more directly infer their learning experiences (and an assessment of learning experiences could help us infer what students are likely to learn). A recent national framework for science standards (National Research Council 2012) moves in this direction by proposing the inclusion of practices of scientists into the standards, not just content knowledge. Practices are largely observable processes.

Of course, assessing processes or practices will require increased specificity in the characterization of practices/processes that can occur on both the social and individual plane. Saying that students engage in "inquiry" is too vague, for both instruction and assessment. There is a growing pocket of research that describes specific social-process constructs relevant to individual processes of learning. For example, Yackel and Cobb (1996) differentiated norms for general classroom discussion from those for mathematical discussion. There are also a growing number of rubrics for describing classroom-level process constructs (e.g., La Paro, Pianta, and Stuhlman 2004).

One particularly interesting case comes from Lindsay Richland, Osnat Zur, and Keith Holyoak (2007). They examined videotapes of mathematics instruction across different nations. They were looking for the use of techniques that helped students draw analogies during instruction—things like gesturing back and forth between examples. The US schools looked different from other nations. The difference was not in the actual number of analogies that teachers introduced. Rather, the difference was that the US teachers did not provide support for making the connections. One might imagine that on assessment of the choice to use analogies to learn, their students would also do relatively poorly.

Focus on Improvement Rather than Proof

The goal of science is to prove. The goal of assessment is to improve. People often forget this. For example, see which answer you would choose to the following complex analogy:

Science : Engineering : Architecture is analogous to : :
(a) Learning Theory : Instruction : Assessment
(b) Assessment : Learning Theory : Instruction
(c) Instruction : Assessment : Learning Theory
(d) Assessment : Instruction : Learning Theory

Our answer is (a). Science is about the causes and consequences of learning. Engineering is about how to use the science of learning to build instruction. Architecture involves deciding what to engineer, which is the implicit role assessments have taken. If you chose answer (b) or (d), you must be a psychometrician.

Oftentimes, the psychometrics of assessment bogs down in proof to the detriment of improvement. In an invited paper written to his peers via the *Journal of Educational and Behavioral Statistics*, Wainer (2010, 12–13) declared, "The psychometrics of today is both more extensive and better than we need. . . . If we want to improve the practice of testing, there is much more bang for the buck to be had in improving tests than improving test theory."

Test evaluation frequently depends on inferential statistics such as t-tests and F-tests, which are designed to (dis)prove a hypothesis. The strict inferential statistics for establishing constructs, reliability, and validity can choke innovation. If we let go of inferential statistics and dreams of proof, we can embrace a new set of *data-mining* tools for handling behavioral data. These tools are exploratory and meant to aid human induction rather than (dis)prove hypotheses. They detect patterns within large data sets, and then it is up to subsequent research to determine if these patterns are valid and reliable. Choice-based assessments are prime candidates for data mining, because they collect large amounts of data by recording each click a student makes while learning.

Industry has already embraced the methodology of analyzing people's choice behaviors on the Internet using data mining (Tancer 2008). Data mining provides a way to search for previously unknown patterns in mountains of data. The patterns can then be put to use. In one apocryphal story (Power 2002), a grocery store chain looked at which items customers tended to purchase together. Many expected pairings cropped up, including milk with cereal and shampoo with conditioner, but one came as a surprise: diapers with beer were often purchased together between 5:00 and 7:00 p.m. It was concluded that fathers sent to the store for diapers rewarded themselves for their errand by buying beer. The grocery store chain responded to this discovery by moving beer nearer to diapers in its stores, boosting sales. Whether or not this legend is true, it illustrates the potential utility of data mining—a computer search discovers unanticipated patterns that are then offered up for human inspection.

One data-mining technique, affinity analysis, yields results that are familiar to anyone who shops at Amazon.com. Amazon knows that customers who buy item A are more likely to buy item B, so it will display item B to customers who are currently looking at item A. Another type of data mining is called classification analysis. An example comes from online gaming. Many online games are free to play but offer in-game purchases, from which the game makers derive the revenue. Most players spend very little on in-game purchases. The revenue comes from "whales": those people who spend freely on upgrades and custom game features. The classification challenge is to identify the whales as early as possible, so that resources can be focused on keeping the whales happy. This is an automated analog of the practice of identifying and catering to whales in gambling—in fact, the term comes from the casino industry.

Data mining provides a new set of tools for handling complex behaviors. Portions of the psychometric community have embraced the challenge of handling rich data. Witness the enthusiastic preface to *Automated Scoring of Complex Tasks in Computer-Based Testing* (Williamson, Mislevy, and Bejar 2006, 2):

> The technological advances of the past decade are a catalyst for change in educational measurement. They allow increased flexibility, complexity, interactivity and realism of computer-administered assessment tasks, including multimedia components. Coupled with capabilities for internet delivery and its implications for large-scale on-demand administration, the potential wealth of data that can be tracked and recorded from such administrations appears capable of revolutionizing assessment. Such a revolution relies, in part, on the promise of a standardized automated analytical approach to measuring previously elusive constructs and complex problem-solving behavior. Of course, this promise depends on the ability of the measurement profession to address new challenges in the practice of educational measurement posed by such an approach to assessment.

This passage nicely captures the situation in which the field of assessment finds itself. There is a good deal of excitement among foundations and researchers. There is a new scholarly society dedicated to educational data mining (http://www.educationaldatamining.org). We share the writers' enthusiasm about the possibilities for the future of data mining, although we do not believe that the pure bottom-up data mining of the industrial examples will work well. Assessment environments need to be designed up-front to help find the telling patterns when there are multiple choices students might make. (We say more about this in chapter 10.)

The danger, from our perspective, is that the field will miss the opportunity of data mining for changing how we think about learning. This would occur if people were to develop data-mining strategies that try to infer students' knowledge. Focusing on knowledge would constitute a mistake similar to that made by those who see in digital media only the potential for "faster and fancier books" (Kendall-Taylor, Lindland, and Mikulak 2010). That is, it would represent a failure to appreciate the opportunity presented by new technologies to shift the paradigm of assessment from the construct of knowledge—a useful proxy for the outcomes of interest in education—to choices—the outcomes of interest themselves.

There are examples of assessments in the psychometric community that are beginning to move away from an exclusive focus on knowledge toward a richer characterization of learning behaviors. One such instance is the Packet Tracer instructional software application used as part of the Cisco Networking Academy (Frezzo et al. 2009). Packet Tracer is a simulation environment that allows users to create and maintain virtual networks of computer routers. This makes it an ideal platform for performance assessments of users' knowledge, skills, and abilities in the domain of router administration. It was designed using the evidence-centered design framework described in chapter 8, and it includes authoring capabilities that allow instructors to design assessment tasks that are ideally suited for their own needs. Packet Tracer is thus exemplary as a cutting-edge knowledge assessment based on logging student data.

Another example of data mining applied to a learning environment comes from the IMMEX Project (Stevens and Thadani 2007). The IMMEX Project hosts an online problem-solving environment replete with various multimedia resources. Each level consists of several related subproblems and a set of learning resources including experimental results, reference materials, and expert (or peer) advice. Students are free to use the resources however they see fit. They may choose to look repeatedly at some resources and ignore others, and they may explore the resources in any order. The students' choices of whether and how to use the resources along with their accuracy on embedded questions are fed into machine-learning algorithms to produce student problem-solving models. Student performances can be characterized in terms of strategies such as guessing (quick, incorrect results with little resource use), perseverating (combing through resources without achieving correct results), plodding (the inefficient use of resources leading to correct results), and expert performance (using only the most useful resources to achieve correct results). The IMMEX Project provides a strong illustration of how it is possible to capture and catalog learning choices in an open environment.

The ability to identify informative patterns of choice will depend on advancements in data mining, which are proliferating quickly. One new technique (Li and Biswas 2002) looks for hidden Markov models (HMM; Rabiner 1989). Automated HMM analysis finds recurrent patterns of choices. (Deriving an HMM is analogous to performing a factor analysis to reveal the underlying structure among the variables, except that in the case of HMMs, the structure is the underlying interaction patterns and sequential transitions among those patterns.) The patterns of interaction are called "hidden" because they do not correspond to any specific choice or transition between states but rather larger patterns of choice. Hogyeong Jeong et al. (2008) used HMM to analyze learner choices using the Teachable Agents software described in chapter 4. (Students teach a computer character, which can then answer questions based on how well it has been taught.) In the Teachable Agent environment used for this research, students could choose from among seven activities at any given time, and they could leave or return to any activity at any time. The goal was to see whether students developed patterns of choice, and whether those patterns predicted future learning.

Figure 9.1 shows the result of an HMM analysis of participants' choices. It revealed three major interaction patterns labeled in figure 9.1 as basic map building (creating the agent's map), map probing (asking the agent to answer questions), and map tracing (asking the agent to explain how it reached its answers). The analysis also computed the probabilities of transitioning from one interaction pattern to another, as indicated by the percentages on the links. The top panel depicts HMM analyses on two different implementations of the Teachable Agent software. The left side represents the choice behavior of children who were given corrective feedback about the quality of the map they were making (e.g., "The correct answer is that algae decrease oxygen"). The right side represents the choice behavior of children who were given tips on what activities they might choose, given a mistake in their map (e.g., "Ask the agent a question, so you can see how it is figuring out the answer"). The specific meaning of the interaction patterns is not relevant to this discussion; what is important to notice is that the two treatments illuminate strikingly different choices for switching between one pattern of activity to another (i.e., the percentages on the arcs).

The bottom panel displays the children's learning choices six weeks later, when students from both conditions learned a new topic. At this time, the corrective feedback and tip feature

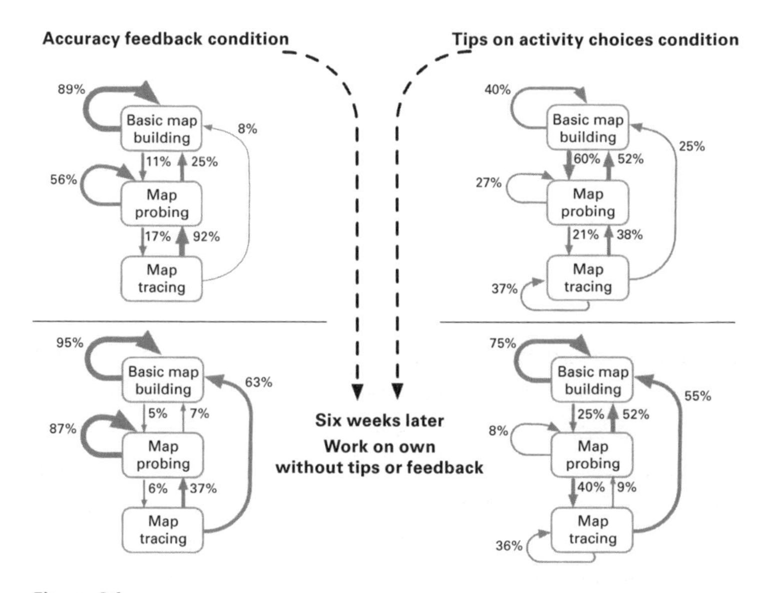

Figure 9.1

A data-mining approach to analyzing choice patterns at initial learning and transfer

Based on a method for deriving HMMs, the top panel shows how students chose to move between various clusters of activities. The percentages represent the probabilities that students transition from one cluster of activities to another. The left side shows the patterns of students who received feedback on their knowledge (accuracy). The right side shows the patterns of students who were given tips on activities that would help them make better learning choices. The bottom panel shows the patterns of choices when students were left to their own devices. The notable aspect is that the choices developed during initial learning transferred when students were choosing on their own to learn a new topic. For example, students in the right panel were much more likely to engage in map tracing.

were turned off, so the children were using identical software to learn the new topic. As may be seen, the choice patterns from initial learning continued, even though the system no longer encouraged one choice pattern over another. The HMM choice analysis thus was able to distinguish and track the effects of the two treatments. Moreover, students who received tips on making learning choices learned more both in the initial learning period and six weeks later (as measured by standard paper-and-pencil tests of knowledge).

Therefore, the story is twofold: data mining can help reveal how choice is a productive framework for assessing the effects of different learning experiences, and learning environments that support choice making lead to better learning. New technologies make architecting and analyzing choice-based assessments a productive line for research and development.

10 A Research and Development Proposal

Building a library of choice-based assessments is a massive undertaking. There are innumerable learning choices one might assess across formal and informal contexts. When high-stakes assessments are built, each new item is vetted extensively, often by administering it to thousands of participants. Yet here we are, proposing the design of a new style of assessment and an accompanying framework that entails untold hundreds of new items. How can we make this a tractable task? The overarching answer is to focus on innovation first, before making the move toward efficiency. So rather than trying to make the perfect assessment, we need to generate a broader set of possibilities. We can prune later.

There are five key challenges. We present them briefly, so the reader can (wisely) choose which challenges and solutions to learn more about in the following subsections.

1. Convince people that assessing learning choices is an interesting enough idea that it is worth pursuing. That is the point of this book.
2. Enlist enough people to work on the problem, so there can be a critical mass of innovative assessments. Our solution is to

help democratize the creation of assessments rather than leave it in the hands of a few.

3. User-test assessment items so that students find them comprehensible and engaging. Current assessments employ a few well-worn scripts: multiple choice, true/false, fill in the blank, short answer, and so on. Everyone knows the scripts, so if a student does poorly, we can assume it is due to their lack of knowledge about the topic and not the test format. With new types of interactive assessments, we want to be sure we are measuring choices about how to achieve a goal instead of measuring aimless meandering dedicated to figuring out the interface. Our solution to this challenge is to create a crowdsourcing platform where it is possible to refine assessments empirically over tens of thousands of users.

4. Validate the choice-based assessments. With standard factual and procedural tests, there is little question whether a given answer is right or wrong. People can rightly ask for the warrant that some choices are better than others, however. To solve this problem, we describe several research methods suitable to formal, informal, and crowdsourcing settings.

5. Decide what to do once an assessment has detected that a student is making poor choices. How do we help students make correct choices and then see if they learn from that instruction? Deciding the best actions we can take to help students learn to make good choices is beyond the purview of this book, but if we want an assessment to yield actionable information, then the assessment should help students, educators, parents, or even a well-programmed computer consider candidate actions. Moreover, assessments that drive instructional actions that measur-

ably improve learning are the strongest possible validation of a learning assessment.

A Platform for Democratizing Assessment Creation

There are many sources of interest and capability for creating assessments tailored to local goals. One possible population of assessment creators comes from a resurgent interest in "merit badges" (Collins and Pea 2011). Groups can develop their own badging system to indicate accomplishment or experience. The reason for the interest is that badges motivate goal setting, pride, and reputation. Badges can also motivate persistence despite the lack of any prospect for material gain, which helps explain the dramatic increase in their use in virtual worlds. Badges, if credible, serve as assessments for those who are trying to decide whether to hire or admit someone (Advanced Placement courses have become badges for admissions to colleges—"I must take lots of AP courses so I can prove that I deserve to be admitted"). We believe there are many people who are interested in creating badge systems, and they could serve as one source of assessment creation.

Members of online communities are another potential source of assessment creators. Gee (2003) describes how online gaming communities develop their own standards and tacit assessments, much like guilds must have done for apprentices and masters. A third great source for assessment development comes from game designers, who build assessments that determine when players can level up. A fourth source is cognitive psychologists. Entry into this profession depends on learning how to craft measures that can detect the effects of subtle experimental manipulations. If you want to be famous in the field, you develop a new method for measuring human beliefs or performance. Surprisingly, this field has not been engaged in the assessment enterprise, but it could be.

We believe there is a great deal of interest in designing assessments. Local experts have a better grasp of what it means to choose well in their domain than do the anonymous people who make so-called drop-in-from-the-sky (DIFTS) assessments. But these experts need tools and resources that facilitate the design of assessments, including the opportunity to gather feedback and see creative, effective examples made by others.

To this end, we are creating a new environment called *Planet OhNo!* Captain Catastrophe and his dog Oops host this environment. The platform is designed for building, refining, and administering assessments to children ranging from fourth to eighth grade. It can be generalized to many ages by changing the overarching narrative and graphic design. The left side of figure 10.1 (plate 4) shows the splash page, which is designed to be inviting for the target age group. The right side of the figure offers a central space that is surrounded by different misadventures. Each misadventure has a number of fanciful disasters waiting to happen (a bear shows up, and your character has just been covered in bear marinade; what do you do?). For each misadventure, there is a set of associated choicelets. A choicelet, as mentioned earlier, is a five- to twenty-minute activity during which students can learn new content, some of which is relevant for solving the misadventures.

The choicelets serve as the primary choice-based assessments. As students complete a choicelet, it is possible to track their choice patterns during learning. Ideally, the choicelets are engaging in their own right. But just in case they are not, the misadventures are fun, and to do well, students can learn how to solve the misadventures by completing the choicelets.

Figure 10.1 (Plate 4)

A platform for crowdsourcing the design of assessments

The left side shows the children's portal into the environment. The right side portrays the main interface where students can access various (assessment) games, accumulate points, and so forth. Through "kidsourcing," students play the assessment games, so it is possible to refine them. The bottom of the figure depicts some of the graphic assets available to anyone who wants to design choice-based assessments in *Planet Ohno!*

The goal of the platform is to make it easy for other people to create choicelets that can be slotted into the adventures. They can attach a choicelet to a misadventure and slot in a "disaster," where students can handle the misadventure using what they learned in the choicelet. Once designers have determined whether their choicelet works, they can decouple it from the system to use it independently for a specific assessment, or they can leave it in the larger environment as one of many assessments.

To help democratize the development of choice-based assessments, we added data collection features. The system includes automatic data logging into a common framework for subsequent analysis by researchers and eventually teachers. There are also security, permission, and log-in schemes that permit various levels of control and access. For instance, it is possible to assign specific misadventures and choicelets to a student. And among other features, researchers can have restricted access to data from their studies.

To help people design usable assessments, we plan to develope an authoring system that makes it easy to create interactive learning environments that collect process data. The authoring system will be of the what-you-see-is-what-you-get variety, much like Adobe Dreamweaver or Microsoft PowerPoint (or even, for those who may remember, Apple's Hypercard system). It will enable people to do layout for various objects (text, graphics, or movies) and define common interactions (e.g., a back button). For the assessment authoring system, there will be an array of built-in libraries for inserting user interactions relevant to assessment. The initial example of a choicelet in chapter 2 uses a catalog that allows students to flip through different color charts. The catalog has a generic data and visual structure, so designers can change the content of each page. It also includes defined data-logging properties, so that it stores important actions (choice of a page) rather than irrelevant actions (position of cursor). *Planet OhNo!* also has a library of graphic assets including characters and backdrops. The bottom of figure 10.1 (plate 4) shows a subset of the characters that populate *Planet OhNo!*

"Kidsourcing" for Refining Assessments

Ideally, with the right set of tools, many people can work on designing assessments. A marketplace of creative and shared assessments would be a nice change from the current situation. One of the most important assets for designing assessments is having people use them. People—lots of people—need to take the assessments so a designer can find out if they are working well. One possible solution is crowdsourcing.

The psychometric community has invested substantial intellectual horsepower to pull forward the logic and statistics of assessments. There has been less attention paid to the design of item formats, with multiple choice, fill in the blank, and occasional essays still being the standard. This is not to say that there has been no attention to creating new assessment formats. Portfolio assessments, for instance, are an innovative format that evaluates student products over a longer timeline.

Choice-based assessments do not follow the usual test scripts. Like all interactive interfaces, they need user testing to ensure that learners understand what they are doing. As good as one's theory might be, there are still a thousand nooks and crannies of decision making that hide beneath the smooth surface of the theory. Designers need empirical data to refine their designs, and for assessment, this means having as many people using the assessment as possible. Enter crowdsourcing.

Crowdsourcing uses massive human power to find novel solutions to complex problems. A well-known example is Wikipedia, which relies on crowds to write and monitor its encyclopedia entries. Yelp! counts on many people to review service providers such as restaurants, painters, and plumbers. Foldit has enlisted hundreds of thousands of players to fold proteins in a spatial game format. The crowd of players has solved biology problems that have defied the computational capabilities of computers and lone scientists (Cooper et al. 2010).

More relevant for our purposes are crowdsourcing approaches such as Amazon.com's Mechanical Turk. MTurk.com is a Web site on which *requesters* post tasks for *workers* to perform for pay. These tasks are often trivial, with correspondingly small pay. For example, workers might be asked to decide whether a word makes them happy or sad, and be paid one penny. More involved tasks need not pay well. Some tasks take up to thirty minutes and pay only fifty cents, but over 16 percent of the workers will still complete such tasks at such pay rates (Buhrmester, Kwang, and Gosling 2011). And workers are plentiful.

For our vision of choice-based assessments, we imagine crowdsourcing assessments for large numbers of children in school classrooms, afterschool programs, museums, or at home for fun. This is one reason that *Planet OhNo!* takes the form of a game. Rather than paying people to use the assessments, we want people to choose to take them. (Plus, why do tests have to be so serious anyway?) If children want to take the assessments, we can use kidsourcing to refine and validate them (the assessments, not the kids). Kidsourcing would provide massive amounts of user data, which could then serve as the fodder for refinement and data-mining analyses that would inform further development and rapid iteration.

A helpful technique for kidsourcing is called *A-B testing*. It is a method of crowdsourcing used by online companies to make small changes to features of their products. For example, Amazon.com (a company that clearly has its act together with respect to data analysis) might show a million customers a page for a certain item. For half of them, the page shows a red button, and for the other half, the page shows a green button. If more customers who see the green button buy the item, Amazon learns that the green button configuration is more effective. Closer to education, Refraction (http://www.kongregate.com/games/GameScience/refraction) is a novel, game-based approach to designing an optimal learning sequence for fractions. By using A-B testing, the Refraction system can learn the optimal sequencing of the curriculum. After completing problem-type A, for instance, half the students can be sent to problem-set B, while the other half works on problem-set C. Then both groups of students work on problem set D. If the students who completed the A-B sequence do better on D than those who completed the A-C sequence, then there is evidence that the A-B sequence is superior to the A-C one. In the context of designing novel assessment formats, A-B testing would provide a way to find the most effective presentation of the materials before using the assessments for their intended purpose. (We say more about this below.)

Before moving on, we want to press the point for how important crowdsourcing could be for advances in the learning sciences and assessments. The number of learning studies that fail because of unvetted measures is extremely high. Researchers might include a series of questions that are too easy or too hard, so they cannot detect the effect of an instructional treatment. Or the test instructions may include a phrase that participants interpret in unintended ways, so they are actually answering a different question. We once asked a physicist to estimate how he spent his time when doing research studies (Schwartz, Martin, and Chang 2008). He said that 95 percent of his time creating experiments was spent on the measurements. In education schools as well as government organizations there has been a great deal of discussion about the importance of randomized clinical trials along with other logical and statistical aspects of research design. This discussion misses the true bottleneck in research. Though we do not have hard evidence, we are convinced that many more studies of learning fail because of bad measures than because of unanticipated confounds. To avoid the risk of failure, researchers frequently design well-controlled studies that use routine ("safe") measures that continue to measure the wrong outcomes. Crowdsourcing could help alleviate some of the risks of innovating new choice-based measures, because researchers could try out their measures beforehand. If successful, crowdsourcing could enable a new generation of research on learning outcomes.

Validating Assessments

In the normative world of education, we care about "better" and "worse," so it is crucial to make warrants that a particular performance is "better." Knowledge-based assessments rely on objective "right" and "wrong" answers as their criteria for better and worse. Few would argue with the claim that "five" is a worse answer than "four" to the question, "What is two plus two?" But with choices, people may reasonably challenge whether one choice is better than another. Who is to say that persisting is better than not? Here we present some approaches to validating whether some choices are better or worse. As always, our criteria of better and worse are with respect to learning. We begin with the correlational approach that we used for the choicelet described in chapter 2 (*Ohno! Has Talent*). Then we describe an experimental approach and conclude with ways to use crowdsourcing.

The top panel of figure 10.2 shows the approach we took for *Ohno! Has Talent.* In this game, students had to make choices about how to learn so they could solve a series of puzzles about mixing light beams to make different colors. The analysis approach depended on individual differences among children and the correlations of those differences with other measures. We found that individual differences in the way students made choices in *Ohno! Has Talent* predicted about 35 percent of the differences in math class performance among students. Specifically, students who spent time trying to figure out which of several color charts was correct were also doing better in mathematics class. This line of evidence is represented by arc b in

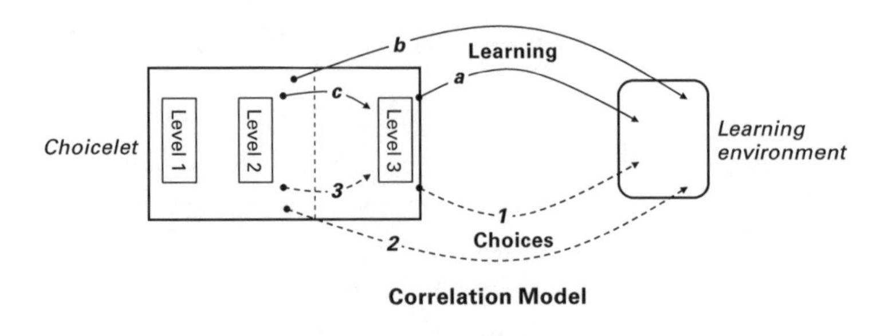

Correlation Model

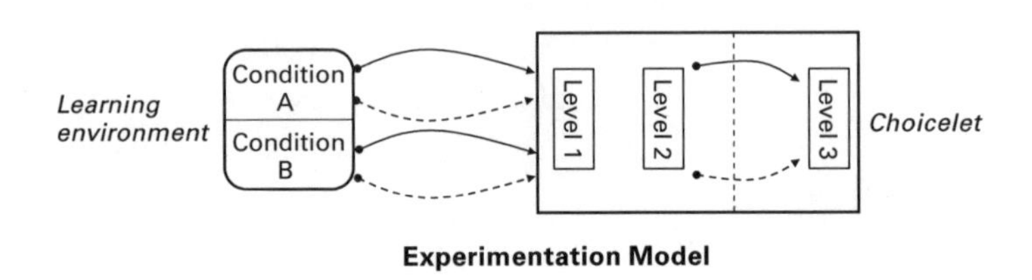

Experimentation Model

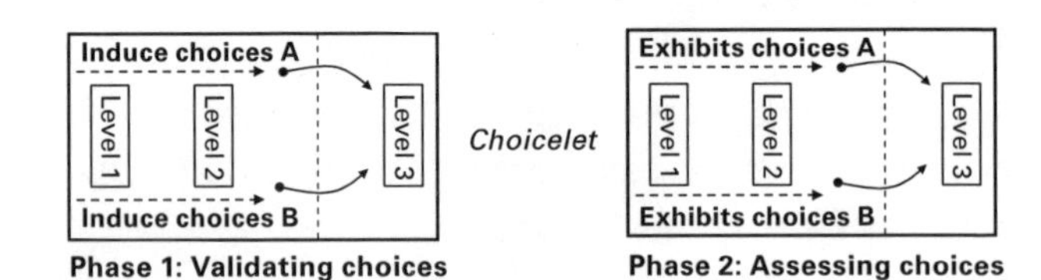

Phase 1: Validating choices **Phase 2: Assessing choices**

Crowdsourcing Model

Figure 10.2

Three validation models

The solid lines indicate evidence that connects choices to standard learning outcomes (correct answers), whereas the dotted lines indicate evidence that connects choices during the assessment to choice-based outcomes.

the top figure. It provides initial support for the claim that certain choices—in this case, the choice to decide which chart to believe—are better for learning.

We can further tighten this line of evidence. For example, the third level of *Ohno! Has Talent* can also be analyzed in figure 10.2 as a posttest for level 2. If students make good learning choices on level 2 and learn about additive color, then they should do well on level 3. It turns out that the same choice pattern in level 2 that predicted learning in students' math class also predicted performance on level 3. Children who chose to evaluate color charts did better on the problems on level 3. This is arc c, and it offers a second line of evidence that the choice to engage in critical thinking is a good learning choice. Finally, we found that student performance on level 3 of the game correlated with how well students were doing in their math class. This is arc a.

In summary, choices in the game predicted children's classroom performance measured by knowledge tests and how well students learned color mixing based on a knowledge assessment embedded as part of the game. The knowledge-based assessment within the third level of *Ohno! Has Talent* also correlated with school performance. This provides a good start in showing that choosing to spend time on deciding what to believe is a good learning choice.

These first three lines of evidence connect choices to standard knowledge-based measures, which is important for convincing those who still think knowledge-based assessments are the ground truth for evaluating learning. Our interest goes further, however, as represented by the dotted lines in figure 10.2.

These lines represent possible evidence that learning choices during the game predict other learning choices. For this line of evidence, it is essential to connect choices within the game to those that occur in other contexts, such as a classroom or informal learning settings.

The results from *Ohno! Has Talent* supplied a further level of detail that could be useful in this regard. There were two dominant patterns of choices in this game. One pattern occurred when students chose to figure out which of the color charts is correct. This predicted better performance in math class. The other pattern happened when students used the experiment room to solve the problems. These students would mix colors in the experiment room to determine which colors to mix for the gameplay. Once they found the answer in the experiment room, they would choose the corresponding color on the game board and mix the right colors. This choice pattern predicted poor performance in math class ($r^2 = -0.15$), even though it was successful in the game. Our speculation is that students who pursued this latter choice pattern had learned to solve problems one at a time rather than trying to find the general explanation. In math class, one can imagine students working to get the right answer for each separate math problem without attempting to find the deeper explanation that handles all possible related problems. The students who spent their time trying to decide which color chart to believe, on the other hand, were trying to find the general framework that could handle any colors in the game.

Given this more refined analysis, we can begin to imagine what types of learning choices we would look for in classrooms. In a situation of collaborative learning, for instance, we might expect the students who solved the problems one at a time to simply ask for the right answer to math problems. In contrast, children who evaluated the catalogs might be expected to spend more time evaluating the rationale of their collaborator's solutions to determine whether to believe them.

We also found evidence tying good choices within the game (arc 3). Choices in the first levels of the game predicted the choices that students made in the last level of the game. Alas, we have not yet looked at math class choices outside the game, so we do not have evidence one way or another regarding arcs 1 and 2. Of course, few assessments achieve the level of ground truth validation where performance on a test is directly correlated to learning behaviors and experiences in school. Most assessments instead assume that students have been exposed to the content in the classroom. The exposure is taken as a constant, and therefore, the inference is that the assessment is measuring the ground truth of what children *should* have learned.

More generally, a correlation approach is not ideally suited to finding how the choices in a choicelet manifest themselves in the world beyond. This is because it would be too inefficient to search across hours of observations to find, catalog, and count choices that might correlate with the choice behaviors in the choicelet. The experimental approach in the middle panel of figure 10.1 (plate 4) is a more tractable methodology.

In the experimental model, there would typically be an intervention where different groups of students are led to make different choices during learning. For example, imagine math class X learns to use a specific mathematical formula by evaluating which company is telling the truth in its advertising. Math class

Y learns the same mathematical formula, and then is asked to use it to compute the values for a set of companies, but without the cover story of evaluating which companies are telling the truth. Sometime afterward, the students from both groups complete *Ohno! Has Talent.* It seems unlikely they would transfer knowledge of the math formula to help solve this particular game. So in this case, one would predict that neither class would show a knowledge arc from the classroom to the assessment. (To achieve this arc, instruction would have to be relevant to color.) On the other hand, one might anticipate that class X would be more likely to choose to apply critical thinking to the color charts in the catalog, whereas class Y would be less likely to do so. If true, this would help make a tight connection between the learning experiences in the classroom and the choices made in the assessment. Moreover, students who choose to evaluate the color charts should learn more from *Ohno! Has Talent,* as measured by the arcs into level 3 of the game. This overall pattern of evidence would indicate that learning to evaluate in school improves students' choices and learning as measured by the assessment. A similar logic can be used to evaluate informal learning experiences, for example, to determine if visiting a museum or completing an outdoor camp subsequently leads to different choices and learning compared to not visiting the exhibit or completing the camp.

This experimental model is the standard approach when evaluating whether some form of instruction (whether about choices or not) is better or worse than another one. It neatly complements our overall interest in using assessments to sort learning experiences rather than sorting students. The result of this type of research can indicate which form of instruction is better as well as when a specific pattern of choice leads to better learning.

The kidsourcing model shown in the bottom panel of figure 10.2 is a hybrid of the experimental and correlational approaches. It provides a way to validate that some choices are better than others for learning, even when it is impossible to find out who the test takers are in the "real world." One approach involves a two-step process. The first step is experimental. It uses A-B testing. The kidsourcers log into the game and receive one of two variations of the choicelet. Each variation "induces" learners into different patterns of choice, perhaps through the manipulation of points or entertainment value. For instance, with *Ohno! Has Talent,* students may be induced to use the experiment room by making use of the chart catalog cost points, and vice versa for inducing students to use the chart catalog. After confirming that students made the anticipated choices in their respective versions, it is then possible to see which students learned about color better. If the students who used the chart catalog did better, then there would be a warrant that this is a better choice pattern.

The second step involves the correlational model. New students use the same choicelet without any inducements. If the assessment is working, students who choose to evaluate the catalog chart should learn more than students who do not do so. Because the experimental approach showed a direct connection between the choices and learning, the correlational results are less prone to arguments that there is no causal relation between the choices and the learning. Thus, even though we do not know much about the kidsourcers, it is still possible to use them to help design assessments. Once the assessment has been developed, it can then be deployed in more typical measurement scenarios such as comparing two forms of instruction.

A second example may be useful. Steven Dow and his colleagues (2010) did an experiment with undergraduates on design skills. There were two conditions in this study: serial and parallel design. Students in the serial condition were induced to design a Web advertisement for a magazine by repeating five design-feedback cycles. They created a design and received generic feedback ("good design uses color well"), then had an opportunity to create their next design, and so on. After their iterations, they created their final advertisement. In the parallel condition, students were induced to design three advertisements first and then got generic feedback on the trio. The students then produced two advertisements and got feedback, and then the final advertisement. In both conditions, the feedback was generic as opposed to specific to their designs, and both designed a total of six advertisements, so the main difference was whether they produced their first few advertisements serially or in parallel. The results demonstrated that students in the parallel condition produced better advertisements. One measurement asked experts to rate the advertisements, and on average, they rated the parallel condition ads as more creative and effective. The second measure is a more interesting assessment.

In a rare opportunity for ground truthing an assessment, the researchers posted the participants' advertisements online, so that different casual users of the Web would see different versions. For example, one segment of Web users got to see the advertisement from one participant, while another segment got to see the ad from a different participant. Using Google analytics, the researchers tracked how often casual Web browsers clicked on each advertisement to actually go to the magazine's Web site. By the end of fourteen days, over one million people had seen an advertisement designed by the participants in the study. As it turned out, the ads from the students in the parallel condition received more "click-through" to the magazine's home page. The researchers thus were able to test the ground truth of parallel versus serial design choices by seeing which of the resulting advertisements were actually more effective. Hearteningly, the crowd and the expert evaluation reached the same conclusion.

This design study gathered evidence that the parallel pattern of choices is better for learning to make a good advertisement. (When people design serially, they tend to refine one idea. When people design multiple versions in parallel, they are more likely to explore the creative possibilities before refining.) The next step, which has not been completed, is to conduct the individual-differences (correlational) phase, in which students would complete the design task without any inducements, so the assessment evaluates their design-feedback choices. Do they choose serial feedback or the more effective parallel approach? In terms of building evidence for the "betterness" of the parallel choice, people who choose the parallel approach should also exhibit better advertisements on average, as evaluated by experts or click-through rates when posted on the Internet.

Choice-Adaptive Instruction

Perhaps the best validation of an assessment would be to show that it provides actionable information that improves learning.

If an assessment helps improve learning, then we know the assessment is measuring something useful and in a useful way. People do try to use assessment information to improve learning—for example, by holding school financing decisions and employees accountable to the assessment. But this produces an indirect connection between an assessment and improving learning; it is hard to use the effects of financing decisions as evidence regarding the quality of the assessment itself. A more direct approach is to match the precision of the assessment to precise changes in learning. If an assessment supplies feedback that a student is making poor choices, and it also includes successful provisions for improving those choices, then it gains a tremendous amount of credibility.

In a computer learning environment, an ideal choice-based assessment would adapt to the choices the students make, so it would support their abilities to make better choices. We will call this a choice-adaptive learning environment. The term *adaptive*, as used here, does not refer to current versions of computer-adaptive testing. In computer-adaptive testing, the term adaptive indicates the ability of the computer to efficiently hone in on a student's level of knowledge by constantly recalibrating question difficulty based on the student's performance so far. Computer-adaptive testing is about shortening overall test-taking time. A choice-adaptive environment instead adapts to students' choices to help guide them to better ones. Instruction and assessment would be seamlessly coupled, providing important guidance to learners, educators, and policymakers.

To develop a choice-adaptive environment will require a new class of behavioral research. There are already computer science techniques for creating intelligent environments that adapt to learners (e.g., Koedinger and Anderson 1997). What is missing, besides new types of assessments, is research on how to effectively guide learning choices. For instance, if an intelligent computer system detects that students are making a poor pattern of choices, what should it do to guide the students to make better choices? Perhaps it should force the learners to make better choices by turning off all the other choices. Maybe it should simply tell the learners the preferred choices. It could incentivize the better choices with points. It could tell the students that other people using the system are making different choices that seem to be working. All of these would likely work to some degree. What we do not know is whether the choice pattern the students are "encouraged" to use would transfer. For example, turning off all the bad choice alternatives would ensure that students make the right choices within the system, but it is not obvious that they would then make the good choices when they return to a world with many choices available. Except for a few instances (e.g., the study by Jeong and colleagues [2008] using HMM described at the end of chapter 8), researchers have not looked at a choice as an outcome, and therefore, we do not know how to help students learn to make good choices.

Summary

This chapter proposed several practical and methodological ideas for how to move forward in making as well as validating new forms of assessments. Many of the precise concerns of psychometrics have been set aside. Our proposal is that new technological possibilities have created a time when it is better to support proliferation. Pruning to technical specifications can occur later through a process of continual improvement. Our generate-and-test proposal is different from current models of assessment development, which seem to be more committed to cultivating a perfect flower that is like all other flowers, but maybe a little more resilient.

V The End Matters

11 Fairness and Choice

Assessment is inextricably linked to questions of fairness. Three outstanding issues are the content of the assessment, the use of the results, and respect for the persons being assessed. Regarding the content of an assessment, educational assessment entails a commitment to elevating some aspects of experience and individuals over others. This in turn raises questions of what measures are fair to include or exclude. As a concrete example, one of us (Schwartz) taught in a remote little Alaskan village for many years (remote, that is, from the vantage point of city dwellers). The village did not have radio or television; it was also five hundred air miles from the nearest road. One year, the students received a reading test that used the word *curb*. The village had no curbs, and most of the students had never seen one. On that item, they surely did poorly compared to city dwellers. This example fits into a larger discussion about whether assessments should take into account students' opportunity to learn (Moss et al. 2008) or should be treated more like driving tests, where the public only cares whether a person is competent to a standard.

In addition to questions about what gets measured, the fairness of a test involves the way it is put to use. For example, in this particular Alaskan school, the lack of item fairness did not really matter, because the principal (not from the village) liked to change student answers. Sitting in his office, he would erase student answers on the bubble forms and insert his own. While this behavior seems perverse, it was his way of putting the assessment to fair use. He made it so that half the students would do so poorly that they would receive federal funding for special needs, and the other half would do so well that they would also receive federal funding for being gifted and talented. (No average students at this school!) He thought this was fair, because these students lived in a village that needed more resources to achieve educational equality. While extreme, the example highlights that the best attempts to build fairness into a test are prone to distortion. People will always work to find advantage when an assessment has material consequences. They may teach to the test, or as in this case, cheat to the test.

Finally, the administration of assessments needs to be fair in the way it respects those people who are taking the test. In the case of the Alaskan school, the doctored tests led many students to be labeled as learning disabled. While this may have been fair at the level of bringing more funds to the school and compensating for unfair test content, it was unfair to these students. Respect for persons is typically handled through some form of informed consent to ensure that people know what they are getting into when they agree to take an assessment.

Choice-based assessments make it more difficult to hide from questions of fairness. If we assess people's choices, then we are making a claim that students should make certain choices. Knowledge-based assessments feel safer. Knowledge can be conceptualized as an enabler. Knowledge is an engine of human performance, but it is still up to the driver to choose where to steer the car. With choices, we are telling people where they should steer their cars. Choice-based assessments go beyond measuring enablement to measuring action itself. This potentially intrudes on personal freedom, because people should be allowed to steer their own car. Of course, knowledge-based assessments also steer the car (as we will discuss below). But choice makes the intrusion more salient. This elevation of ethical concern is notable, since it shows that choices are closer to what people care about and therefore what we should be assessing.

We examine the three fairness issues in turn: the selection of what choices to evaluate, the use of assessments to enforce patterns of choice, and respect for those who take the tests. Again, we do not believe these fairness issues are unique to choice-based assessments, but choice makes them more apparent. Our goal is to raise these issues and some of their dimensions. Readers should not read this chapter if they are expecting answers. If readers plan to create or deploy assessments, though, it is useful to explore the ethical dimensions of the endeavor.

Deciding Which Choices to Assess

When measuring students' knowledge, there is a belief that the knowledge is objective. Here, we do not mean an objective measure of how much knowledge the student has but rather the notion of objective knowledge. For example, knowledge that the earth orbits the sun is taken as objective. Whether or not it is true, the knowledge is so broadly shared and accepted that it is understood as objective. Disciplines have well-established criteria for what comprises the knowledge in their field. Choice is another matter.

Choice is manifestly a social construction. What constitutes a choice for one person may not be a choice for another. Hazel Markus (personal communication) described a study where the participants were led to the door of a room in which they were to fill out a short survey. The room had five substations, in each of which were five colored pencils, five sheets of paper that held the same questionnaire, and five candies. Once the participants were done, the experimenter asked how many choices they had made. East Indians said they made about one or two choices (choosing among colored pencils was not really a choice). Americans on average said they made four. One woman said she had made nine choices. For instance, she had picked up one of the candies, set it down on second thought, and picked up another candy; to her, this constituted three separate choices.

This raises the question of what choices to elevate into "real choices" through assessments. We probably do not want to make all possible choices meaningful. As Barry Schwartz (2004) demonstrated, too many choices can cause people unhappiness, especially if the individuals are perfectionists. At the same time, people can benefit from learning about choices they never knew were available as well as their mostly likely outcomes.

The social construction of choice raises issues of fairness. If some choices are not recognized by a segment of the population, do we have the right to make those choices central to their education, and if we do, will we intrude on other choices they value more? We confront a similar problem when deciding what "knowledge" to include in a history curriculum. Should a treatment of the United States, say, include the Anglo-Saxon version of America, the Native American version, the African-American version, or perhaps the Soviet one? Notably, these types of issues do not show up much in science or mathematics curricula (e.g., Should we teach intelligent design?). With the introduction of choice as an outcome, educators in the science, technology, engineering, and mathematics disciplines would no longer be falsely protected from these normative questions by believing that whatever they teach is safely objective. If they were teaching choices, then they could not ignore the socially constructed reality of educational outcomes. They would have to consider whether asking students to develop interest and persistence has equal standing to learning the objectively known quadratic equation.

How might we decide what choices to emphasize while minimizing the potential for unfairness? It is important to remember that the choices we care about are learning-relevant ones; not all choices are diagnostic from the perspective of learning. A useful first step is to take an empirical approach. Here, the goal would be to determine which choices have the largest influence on learning. If we were to analyze the log file of a student using *Ohno! Has Talent*, for example, the choice of where to let the cursor rest while thinking is less relevant than the choice of whether to open up one of the color charts. A data-driven answer would help alleviate some of the problems associated with the social construction of what constitutes a useful choice, at least with respect to learning. People would then be able to debate whether the learning value of a choice is high enough that it is worth favoring in assessment.

A complementary approach is to look for a set of learning choices that most people would accept, if they understood the underlying rationale. Jim Greeno (forthcoming) has taken this approach by reviewing work on *intellectual virtues*. He highlights that elements of moral behavior can be found in intellectual pursuits: patience, open-mindedness, responsibility, the fair evaluation of arguments, and so on. A rational analysis of such intellectual virtues could provide a high-level framework for making decisions about which choices fall within the purview of the intellectual pursuit of education. Assertions about the appropriateness of measuring one choice or another could be made by reference to a constitution of intellectual virtues. (No doubt, there would also need to be a bill of rights.)

The Use of Assessments to Enforce Choices

Our hope is that choice-based assessments can be used to help students develop good learning choices that will serve their interests well. The logic is that if assessments focus on choices, then instruction will try to instill those choices. This raises the unhappy paradox that to help students learn to choose for themselves, it may be necessary to shape their choices, which would mean they were never "really" choosing.

Eamonn Callan (2009) describes a version of the paradox in his essay on choosing to be Catholic. The dilemma is that deep Catholic faith requires that one choose to be a Catholic, but the only way one can truly choose Catholicism is if one has sufficient knowledge to understand what is being chosen. The question is: Should parents deny their children the choice of not being Catholic when they are young, so that the children can gain the requisite knowledge for a future free choice on becoming Catholic? These are deep theoretical waters. Of course, choice-based assessments are not the only educational endeavors that float on them. Education is normative, and forces larger than the learner conspire to deem what is worth learning—whether this involves knowledge or choice.

One way to try to address the paradox is to make it into an instructional question. Perhaps there is a way to make instruction where students have the opportunity to make decisions freely, and then they can experience the consequences. They thus can judge whether they like those consequences, which would help them learn about the value of different types of choices. This is a good approach to learning, because experiencing the results of one's choices is an excellent way to learn. Education can provide a protected environment to ensure that the choices do not have catastrophic outcomes—a choice sandbox in which students can learn about different choices and their effects. This does not skirt the paradox of enforcing choices, as we will explain next, but it may provide a useful compromise.

Providing students with the belief they are making a choice does not skirt the paradox because the outcomes of those choices and how those outcomes shape future choices are still enforced by authority. In educational settings, the consequences of making a given choice are largely orchestrated by that setting. This is how educational settings can create a protected learning environment: by controlling the consequences attached to different choices. This orchestration also makes it so that some choices are better than others. So while children may believe they have agency in the choices they make, forces outside their control are still shaping them—forces that educators have explicitly or implicitly designed.

B. F. Skinner (1986), a US behaviorist, famously proposed that education should unambiguously shape student behavior by establishing clear reinforcement contingencies for those things that need to be taught. School is not life, he contended. After school, students can choose—or more properly, believe they choose—whatever actions they would like. Skinner's arguments are compelling, although the science behind them has been superseded by new findings and theories. But at a higher level, Skinner missed something fundamental. The narrative of choice and agency is basic to contemporary discourse and people's self-conception (Bandura 1989). Whether or not the narrative is correct, agency is a socially constructed reality, and our civil society depends on it. Students need to experience and reflect on the agency of choice, even if they are guided toward some choices over others. So whether or not one likes the idea of providing "faux" choices for students, it is important for them to experience choice making. In Callan's paradox, we would be satisfied if children had a chance to entertain the possibility of not being Catholic, even if that was not really an option until they were older. If the goal is to prepare people to choose, then the existence of choices needs to suffuse learning.

Respect for People's Right to Choose

By collecting student choices, we are looking for patterns that tell us about learners and their learning experiences. To what extent should the learners (and their parents) have the right to choose to participate, and to what degree do they need to know the details of what they are choosing and how their results will be used?

In the conduct of federally funded research, the rules for respecting people's rights are enforced. To experiment or gather data on human behavior, researchers need to submit their research protocol to a local institutional review board. This board is entrusted with protecting the rights of human subjects, and it is under the broader regulation of a federal body. In addition to questions of risk and confidentiality, a major component of any review is whether and how the participants give informed consent. Informed consent means that the participants understand what they are agreeing to with respect to both the experience itself and the potential uses of their data. There are conditions under which informed consent is not required, but a lack of transparency needs to be well justified and pose minimal risk to the participants.

Oftentimes, decisions about informed consent intersect with practical considerations. School districts in California use passive consent to administer assessments. Passive consent means that parents do not have to give their approval for their children to take a test, but the parents can always withdraw their implied consent if they do not want their children to be tested. The schools do not work hard to inform parents that they can withdraw their consent. One practical reason is that absentee students are counted as "fails" in the school's overall score. Children who do not take the tests lower the standing of the school.

This seems like a bizarre policy for evaluating a school—punishing the school for families who choose against a test. Yet the scoring policy has a history. Before the policy, some schools were asking their least capable students to stay home, so they would not take the test. This way, the low-achieving students would not bring down the average of the school. The absentee policy of counting missing students as fails was put in place to stop schools from doing this. With the new policy, schools do not broadly publicize that students are not compelled to take high-stakes tests, because students who do not take the test necessarily reduce the school average. Practical considerations have trumped the subtleties of informed consent. It is notable that this example is eerily close to that of the Alaskan principal, who simply changed answers to gain material advantage for his school. When there are material consequences, people will frequently interpret what fair means in self-serving ways.

Because assessments cannot guarantee they are fair, informed consent becomes especially significant when assessment data are used to make decisions about future opportunities and other material impacts. The people who have the strongest claim to informed consent are those who will be affected. When the assessments are being used to evaluate learning experiences, as we advocated earlier, then it is not clear where to get informed consent. One answer is that if the assessments are being used to evaluate the educators who create the learning experiences, then respect for the educators would dictate that they understand what is going on and the possible uses of the data. Of course, the fact that educators are informed does not mean that their consent is voluntary. The consent could be a tacit (or explicit) element of their employment.

A less pressing aspect of informed consent, at least in our opinion, involves letting students know that they are taking an assessment. In our *Ohno! Has Talent* example, students thought they were playing a game. They thought the goal was to level up in a game about mixing colors. They did not know that our intent for the game was to measure their learning choices involving critical thinking. At the time, it never occurred to us to tell them. Is this fair? Our current thinking, as unsatisfying as it will be, is that the demands of transparency can be mitigated by practical concerns, assuming there is minimal risk or consequence to those being assessed.

Some researchers have advocated "stealth" assessments, where students do not know they are being tested (Shute 2011). One benefit of stealth assessments is that they can be ongoing rather than highly marked events. With an assessment, we usually want to know a learner's *typical performance*—what they are choosing most of the time. Thus, ongoing measurement provides a sufficient sample to determine typical choice behaviors.

In contrast, when students know they are being tested, they often strive for *maximal performance*. For instance, students complete test preparation classes so they can do well on admissions tests. The assessment in this case is not measuring what learners are typically like but instead what the learners are like when giving maximal effort (which they may or may not do most other times). Moreover, the assessments end up favoring those who have the resources to take test preparation classes to enhance their maximal performance, while measuring the typical performances of those who do not attend such courses.

Transparency thus can make it difficult to interpret test results, and in the case of high-stakes tests, it can actually make tests less fair by one interpretation.

Transparency also leads to "gaming" a test. Students put in maximal effort to learn how to pass a test without actually learning the content in any deep way. We think choice-based assessments can avoid some of the gaming problem, because students need to learn during the test. If they gamed the test by learning about which choices help them learn, that would be an excellent outcome. But one can imagine that students might instead learn that they should make certain choices to do well on the test and not learn anything. So a lack of transparency, at least about specific test items, seems warranted, though we imagine that there are those who will disagree by claiming students have a right to know exactly what will be on the test and when the test is being given.

Summary

People have a natural tendency toward wishful thinking. Wishful thinking about assessments—that they are impartial measures, much like a yardstick is an impartial measure of height—lets people avoid the clutter of ethical questions and treat assessments as objective measures. But the truth is that an educational assessment is not a yardstick. It does not simply measure a learning outcome. Assessment elevates some aspects of experience over others, and it actively shapes what people consider important. Assessments do not merely test reality; they also create it.

Assessments are intended to help students, educators, parents, institutions, and policymakers formulate decisions with consequences as well. In combination, the reality- and decision-making aspects of assessment raise issues of fairness about an assessment's content and use. On the assumption that normative assessments can never be fully fair, assessments also raise questions about the degree to which test takers need to understand these matters before consenting to be tested. These are difficult questions, and our goal is not to reach answers. Rather, our aim is to help people avoid wishful thinking, so that those who join in to help work on assessments will keep these matters in mind.

12 Final Summary

A wry professor of clinical psychology once told us, "I do diagnosis, not treatment." Her research involved defining clinical levels of psychological dysfunctions and tracking down their etiology. She did not study how to fix the dysfunction. She saw herself as a basic scientist, not an applied one. Oftentimes, assessment work has the same characteristic, where the accepted goal is to diagnose (or characterize) learners. It is up to other people to figure out what to do, whoever those other people might be. This misses the basic fact that educational assessment is applied work from the outset.

The purpose of assessment is normative. The goal is to improve, not prove. For the professor, if two measures yielded the same diagnosis at the same cost, it would be silly to ask whether one is preferable. In education, the same logic does not apply, because assessments are not passive measures. They shape what people believe is useful and therefore influence the actions that individuals and governments undertake. If measuring breath-holding capacity worked better than the SAT for predicting college success, it would still be a mistake to use breath holding as an assessment. Test preparation programs would focus on the ability to hold one's breath. Assessments have social consequences, and as such, the design of assessment goes beyond pure scientific measurement.

For many, assessments are a lighthouse in the fog of education—a clear guide by which to make safe decisions. But in reality, assessments create the fog. Current assessments perpetuate beliefs that the proper outcomes of learning are static facts and routine skills—stuff that is easy to score as right or wrong. Interest, curiosity, identification, self-efficacy, belonging, and all the other goals of informal learning cannot even sit at the assessment table, because these outcomes are too far removed from current beliefs about what is *really* important. Assessments seem to be built on the presupposition that people will never need to learn anything new after the test, because current assessments miss so many aspects of what it means to be prepared for future learning. These frozen-moment assessments have influenced what people think counts as useful learning, which then shows up in curricula, standards, instructional technologies, and people's pursuits.

If the fog were lifted, we would see that most of the stakeholders in education care first and foremost about people's abilities to make good choices. Making good choices depends on what people know, but it also depends on much more, including interest, persistence, and a host of twenty-first-century soft skills that are critical to learning. Where we can anticipate a stable future—decoding letters into words is likely to be a stable demand for the next fifty years—then knowledge- and skill-based assessments make sense. In relation to those aspects of the future that are less stable, though, people will need to choose whether, what, when, and how to learn. Hence, it is important to focus on choices that influence learning, and assessments should measure those choices. Choice is the critical outcome of learning, not knowledge. Knowledge is an enabler; choice is the outcome.

Assessing choices during learning has a number of attractive properties. Foremost, choice-based assessments are process oriented. They examine learning choices in action rather than only the end products. This process focus makes it possible to connect the learning behaviors during the assessment to processes that occur in a learning environment. Second, the assessments reveal what students are prepared to learn, so they are prospective as opposed to retrospective. Third, choice resonates with the rest of the social sciences that examine the movements of people, money, and ideas. Fourth, choices do not lend themselves to simplistic reifications whereby things like people's knowledge or personality traits are misinterpreted as independent of context and immune to change. Fifth, choices can measure a much greater range of learning outcomes than fact retrieval and procedural application. We have demonstrated several, including persistence after failure, critical thinking, attending to some ideas over others, creating a general solution, creative design, reading to learn, use of help, inductive strategies, and the uptake of feedback. There are many more to be had. Sixth, learning choices are a good candidate for inclusion in standards, which currently define what knowledge students should have but stay strangely silent about the processes of learning themselves.

Recent advancements in technology create a special opportunity for moving toward a new paradigm of assessment. There are risks, however. People may only use technology to make us faster and more entrenched at doing the wrong thing. If used well, technology makes it possible to create and validate choice-based assessments by using the rapid generation of interactive environments, crowdsourcing, automated logging, and data mining. To create choice-based assessments, we have proposed a strategy that puts assessment development in the hands of many in a process of continual improvement. Rather than assuming there is a dark priesthood of assessment makers who pray at the altar of psychometrics, we have suggested democratizing assessment design to generate as many instances as possible. We should prune after, not before, the assessments are created. High variability is the route to innovation; a press toward efficiency is not.

We have described one possible approach to support rapid development with the example of *Planet OhNo!*—an example that included resources for designing and evaluating candidate assessments. We have also offered a number of methodological strategies for helping people determine whether they are identifying choices that are better or worse. Most notably, we advocated assessment approaches that work to evaluate learning experiences. This changes the focus of assessments. Instead of making a scientific diagnosis of an individual, for which there may or may not be a treatment, we have proposed diagnosing the learning experiences themselves, because this is what needs to change for broad-scale improvements in learning.

We have concluded with a reminder that the assessment enterprise must be constantly attentive to questions of fairness. Because assessment is normative, it raises issues of fairness that science normally does not. Choice-based assessments bring these fairness considerations into strong relief because they explicitly favor some choices over others. In this regard, choice-based assessments make us squeamish. It would be easier to hide behind the idea that we are teaching students the truth and innocently measuring whether they have learned it. The queasiness we feel about making decisions regarding which choices are better and worse indicates that we are getting closer to the proper concerns of education.

Notes

1. The mystery operator is a form of modular multiplication, with P as 1, Q as 2, and so on. P is thus the "identity" element: P crossed with any letter yields that letter. R crossed with a letter yields "three times" that letter in modular or "clock" counting; for example, R crossed with Q yields Q, because Q is 2 and R is 3, and $3 \times 2 = 6$, and $6 \bmod 4 = 2$, which is Q.

2. It is possible that the graduate students had a propensity to create visual representations of data prior to graduate school, in which case they did not learn to do so during graduate school. In this alternative account, the propensity is what caused them to go to graduate school in the first place. On this interpretation, the diagnosis task would make a great admissions test, given that 100 percent of the graduate students constructed visualizations. Of course, if the diagnosis task were used as an admissions test, only 18 percent of undergraduates from Stanford would be admitted, which seems unlikely. Our suspicion is that students learned to choose to make visualizations because of graduate school, not as a precondition for going to graduate school.

References

Anderson, J. R. 2000. *Cognitive Psychology and Its Implications*. 5th ed. New York: Worth.

Anderson, K. T., S. J. Zuiker, G. Taasoobshirazi, and D. T. Hickey. 2011. "Classroom Discourse as a Tool to Enhance Formative Assessment and Practice in Science." *International Journal of Science Education* 29:1721–1744.

Anderson, R. C., and P. D. Pearson. 1984. "A Schema-Theoretic View of Basic Processes in Reading." In *Handbook of Reading Research*, ed. P. D. Pearson, R. Barr, M. L. Kamil, and P. Mosenthal, 255–291. White Plains, NY: Longman.

Appelbaum, E., and R. Batt. 1994. *The New American Workplace*. New York: ILR Press.

Arena, D. A. 2012. "Commercial Video Games as Preparation for Future Learning." PhD diss., Stanford University.

Arena, D., and D. L. Schwartz. 2010. Stats Invaders! Learning about Statistics by Playing a Classic Video Game. In *Proceedings of the Fifth International Conference on Foundations of Digital Games*, ed. I. Horswill and Y. Pisan, 248–249. New York: ACM.

Baker, R.S.J.d., S. Gowda, and A. Corbett. 2011. "Automatically Detecting a Student's Preparation for Future Learning: Help Use Is Key." In Proceedings of the Fourth International Conference on Educational

Data Mining, ed. M. Pechenizkiy, T. Calders, C. Conati, S. Ventura, C. Romero, and J. Stamper, 179–188. Eindhoven, Netherlands.

Bandura, A. 1989. "Human Agency in Social Cognitive Theory." *American Psychologist* 44, no. 9:1175–1184.

Barab, S. A., and J. A. Plucker. 2002. "Smart People or Smart Contexts? Cognition, Ability, and Talent Development in an Age of Situated Approaches to Knowing and Learning." *Educational Psychologist* 37, no. 3:165–182.

Barnett, S. M., and S. J. Ceci. 2002. "When and Where Do We Apply What We Learn? A Taxonomy for Far Transfer." *Psychological Bulletin* 128:612–637.

Barron, F., and D. M. Harrington. 1981. "Creativity, Intelligence, and Personality." *Annual Review of Psychology* 32:439–476.

Bell, P., B. Lewenstein, A. W. Shouse, and M. A. Feder, eds. 2009. *Learning Science in Informal Environments: People, Places, and Pursuits*. Committee on Learning Science in Informal Environments, Board on Science Education, Center for Education, Division of Behavioral and Social Sciences and Education, National Research Council. Washington, DC: National Academies Press.

Benner, C. 2002. *Work in the New Economy: Flexible Labor Markets in Silicon Valley*. Oxford: Blackwell Publishing.

Biederman, I., and M. M. Shiffrar. 1987. "Sexing Day-Old Chicks: A Case Study and Expert Systems Analysis of a Difficult Perceptual Learning Task." *Journal of Experimental Psychology: Learning, Memory, and Cognition* 13:640–645.

Black, P., and D. Williams. 1998. "Inside the Black Box: Raising Standards through Classroom Assessment." *Phi Delta Kappan* 80, no. 2:139–148.

Blackwell, L. S., K. H. Trzesniewski, and C. S. Dweck. 2007. "Implicit Theories of Intelligence Predict Achievement across an Adolescent Transition: A Longitudinal Study and an Intervention." *Child Development* 78, no. 1:246–263.

Blair, K. 2009. "The Neglected Importance of Feedback Perception in Learning: An Analysis of Children and Adults' Update of Quantitative Feedback in a Mathematics Simulation Environment." PhD diss., Stanford University.

Bransford, J. D., and M. K. Johnson. 1972. "Contextual Prerequisites for Understanding: Some Investigators of Comprehension and Recall." *Journal of Verbal Learning and Verbal Behavior* 11:717–726.

Bransford, J. D., and D. L. Schwartz. 1999. "Rethinking Transfer: A Simple Proposal with Multiple Implications." *Review of Research in Education* 24:61–100.

Broudy, H. S. 1977. "Types of Knowledge and Purposes of Education." In *Schooling and the Acquisition of Knowledge,* ed. R. C. Anderson, R. J. Spiro, and W. E. Montague, 1–17. Hillsdale, NJ: Erlbaum.

Buhrmester, M., T. Kwang, and S. D. Gosling. 2011. "Amazon's Mechanical Turk: A New Source of Inexpensive, Yet High-Quality, Data?" *Perspectives on Psychological Science* 6, no. 1:3–5.

Callan, E. 2009. "Why Bring the Kids into This? McLaughlin and Anscombe on Religious Understanding and Upbringing." In *Faith in Education: A Tribute to Terence MacLaughlin,* ed. G. Haydon. London: London Institute of Education Publications.

Chase, C. C. 2011. "Motivating Persistence in the Face of Failure: The Impact of an Ego-Protective Buffer on Learning Choices and Outcomes in a Computer-Based Educational Game." PhD diss., Stanford University.

Chase, C. C., D. B. Chin, M. A. Oppezzo, and D. L. Schwartz. 2009. "Teachable Agents and the Protégé Effect: Increasing the Effort towards Learning." *Journal of Science Education and Technology* 18:334–352.

Chomsky, N. 1966. *Cartesian Linguistics: A Chapter in the History of Rationalist Thought.* New York: Harper & Row.

Collins, A., and R. Pea. 2011. "The Advantages of Alternative Certifications for Students." *Education Week* 31, no. 8:22–23.

Cooper, S., F. Khatib, A. Treuille, J. Barbero, J. Lee, M. Beenen, A. Leaver-Fay, D. Baker, Z. Popovi⊠, and Foldit players. 2010. "Predicting Protein Structures with a Multiplayer Online Game." *Nature* 446:756–760.

Costa, P. T., Jr., and R. R. McCrae. 1992. *Revised NEO Personality Inventory (NEO-PI-R) and NEO Five-Factor Inventory (NEO-FFI) Manual*. Odessa, FL: Psychological Assessment Resources.

Crocker, L., and J. Algina. 1986. *Introduction to Classical and Modern Test Theory*. New York: Harcourt Brace Jovanovich.

Damasio, A. R. 1994. *Descartes Error: Emotion, Reason and the Human Brain*. New York: G. P. Putnam's Sons.

DeYoung, C. G., J. B. Hirsh, M. S. Shane, X. Papademetris, N. Rajevaan, and J. R. Gray. 2010. "Testing Predictions from Personality Neuroscience: Brain Structure and the Big Five." *Psychological Science* 21:820–828.

Dow, S. P., A. Glassco, J. Kass, M. Schwarz, D. L. Schwartz, and S. R. Klemmer. 2010. "Parallel Prototyping Leads to Better Design Results, More Divergent Creations, and Self-Efficacy Gains." *ACM Transactions on Computer-Human Interaction* 17, no. 4:1–24.

Ericsson, K. A., ed. 2009. *Development of Professional Expertise: Toward Measurement of Expert Performance and Design of Optimal Learning Environments*. New York: Cambridge University Press.

Ericsson, K. A., R. Th. Krampe, and C. Tesch-Römer. 1993. "The Role of Deliberate Practice in the Acquisition of Expert Performance." *Psychological Review* 100:363–406.

Falk, J. H., and L. D. Dierking. 2002. *Lessons without Limit: How Free-Choice Learning Is Transforming Education*. Walnut Creek, CA: AltaMira Press.

Feuerstein, R. 1979. *The Dynamic Assessment of Retarded Performers: The Learning Potential Assessment Device, Theory, Instruments, and Techniques*. Baltimore, MD: University Park Press.

Frezzo, D. C., J. T. Behrens, R. J. Mislevy, P. West, and K. E. DiCerbo. 2009. "Psychometric and Evidentiary Approaches to Simulation Assessment in Packet Tracer Software." *ICNS '09: Proceedings of the Fifth International Conference on Networking and Services*, eds. J. L. Mauri, V. Casares, R. Tomas, T. Serra, and O. Dini, 555–560. Washington, DC: IEEE Computer Society.

Gee, J. P. 2003. *What Video Games Have to Teach Us about Learning and Literacy*. New York: Palgrave.

Ghiselli, E. E. 1966. *The Validity of Occupational Aptitude Tests*. New York: Wiley.

Gibson, J. J., and E. J. Gibson. 1955. "Perceptual Learning: Differentiation or Enrichment." *Psychological Review* 62:32–51.

Gough, H. G. 1979. "A Creative Personality Scale for the Adjective Check List." *Journal of Personality and Social Psychology* 37, no. 8:1398–1405.

Greeno, J. G. Forthcoming. "Framing Intellective Identities, Intellective Characters, and Epistemic Values." In *Educating Comprehensively: Varieties of Educational Experiences*, ed. L. Lin, H. Varenne, and E. W. Gordon. Vol. 3. Lewiston, NY: Edwin Mellen Press.

Gresalfi, M. S. 2009. "Taking Up Opportunities to Learn: Constructing Dispositions in Mathematics Classrooms." *Journal of the Learning Sciences* 18:327–369.

Haertel, E. H., and J. L. Herman. 2005. "A Historical Perspective on Validity Arguments for Accountability Testing." In *Uses and Misuses of Data in Accountability Testing. Yearbook of the National Society for the Study of Education*, ed. J. L. Herman and E. H. Haertel, 104:1–34. Boston, MA: Blackwell Publishing.

Harré, R., and L. van Langenhove, eds. 1999. *Positioning Theory: Moral Contexts of Intentional Action*. Oxford: Blackwell.

Hatano, G., and K. Inagaki. 1986. "Two Courses of Expertise." In *Child Development and Education in Japan*, ed. H. Stevenson, H. Azuma, and K. Hakuta, 262–272. New York: Freeman.

Hatano, G., and K. Osawa. 1983. "Digit Memory of Grand Experts in Abacus-Derived Mental Calculation." *Cognition* 15:95–110.

Ito, M., S. Baumer, M. Bittanti, d. boyd, R. Cody, B. Herr-Stephenson, H. A. Horst, P. G. Lange, D. Mahendran, K. Z. Martinez, C. J. Pascoe, D. Perkel, L. Robinson, C. Sims, and L. Tripp. 2009. *Hanging Out, Messing Around, Geeking Out: Kids Living and Learning with New Media.* Cambridge, MA: MIT Press.

Iyengar, S. S., and M. R. Lepper. 1999. "Rethinking the Value of Choice: A Cultural Perspective on Intrinsic Motivation." *Journal of Personality and Social Psychology* 76:349–366.

Jeong, H., A. Gupta, R. Roscoe, J. Wagster, G. Biswas, and D. L. Schwartz. 2008. "Using Hidden Markov Models to Characterize Student Behaviors in Learning-by-Teaching Environments." *Proceedings of the Ninth International Conference on Intelligent Tutoring Systems*, 614–625.

Kaminski, J. A., V. M. Sloutsky, and A. F. Heckler. 2008. "Learning Theory: The Advantage of Abstract Examples in Learning Math." *Science* 320:454–455.

Kendall-Taylor, N., E. Lindland, and A. Mikulak. 2010. *"Faster and Fancier Books": Mapping the Gaps between Expert and Public Understandings of Digital Media and Learning.* Washington, DC: FrameWorks Institute.

Koedinger, K. R., and J. R. Anderson. 1997. "Intelligent Tutoring Goes to School in the Big City." *International Journal of Artificial Intelligence in Education* 8:30–43.

Konold, C. 1989. "Informal Conceptions of Probability." *Cognition and Instruction* 6, no. 1:59–98.

La Paro, K. M., R. C. Pianta, and M. Stuhlman. 2004. "The Classroom Assessment Scoring System: Findings from the Prekindergarten Year." *Elementary School Journal* 104:409–426.

Lederman, L., with D. Teresi. 1993. *The God Particle: If the Universe is the Answer, What Is the Question?* New York: Houghton Mifflin.

Li, C., and G. Biswas. 2002. "A Bayesian Approach for Learning Hidden Markov Models from Data." *Science Progress* 10:201–219.

Martin, L., and D. L. Schwartz. 2009. "Prospective Adaptation in the Use of Representational Tools." *Cognition and Instruction* 27, no. 4:370–400.

Massa, L. J., and R. E. Mayer. 2006. "Testing the ATI hypothesis: Should multimedia instruction accommodate verbalizer-visualizer cognitive style?" *Learning and Individual Differences* 16:321–336.

McDermott, R. 1993. "Acquisition of a Child by a Learning Disability." In *Understanding Practice*, ed. S. Chaiklin and J. Lave, 269–305. London: Cambridge University Press.

Mislevy, R. J., L. S. Steinberg, and R. G. Almond. 2003. "On the Structure of Educational Assessments." *Measurement: Interdisciplinary Research and Perspectives* 1:3–67.

Moss, P. A., D. C. Pullin, J. P. Gee, E. H. Haertel, and L. J. Young, eds. 2008. *Assessment, Equity, and Opportunity to Learn*. Cambridge: Cambridge University Press.

National Research Council. 2007. *Taking Science to School: Learning and Teaching Science in Grades K–8*. Washington, DC: The National Academies Press.

National Research Council. 2012. *A Framework for K–12 Science Education: Practices, Crosscutting Concepts, and Core Ideas*. Washington, DC: National Academies Press.

Newell, A., and H. A. Simon. 1972. *Human Problem Solving*. Englewood Cliffs, NJ: Prentice-Hall.

Nisbett, R. E., D. Krantz, C. Jepson, and Z. Kunda. 1983. "The Use of Statistical Heuristics in Everyday Inductive Reasoning." *Psychological Review* 90:339–363.

Norris, S. P. 1985. "Synthesis of Research on Critical Thinking." *Educational Leadership* (May):40–45.

Olivier, C., and R. F. Bolwer. 1996. *Learning to Learn.* New York: Fireside.

Ortega y Gasset, J. 1960. What Is Philosophy? Trans. Mildred Adams. new York: W. W. Norton.

Pinker, S. 1994. *The Language Instinct: How the Mind Creates Language.* New York: HarperCollins.

Polyani, M. 1966. *The Tacit Dimension.* Garden City, NY: Doubleday.

Power, D. J. 2002. "What Is the 'True Story' about Data Mining, Beer, and Diapers?" *DSS News* 3, no. 23. http://www.dssresources.com/newsletters/66.php.

Rabiner, L. R. 1989. "A Tutorial on Hidden Markov Models and Selected Applications in Speech Recognition." *Proceedings of the IEEE* 77:257–286.

Rafferty, A. N. 2007. "Using FACT to Challenge Assumptions: Frequency, Accuracy, Choice, and Timing in Machine Learning." Master's thesis, Stanford University.

Reeves, B., and J. L. Read. 2009. *Total Engagement: Using Games and Virtual Environments to Change the Way People Work and Businesses Compete.* Cambridge, MA: Harvard Business Press.

Resnick, D. P., and L. B. Resnick. 1994. "Performance Assessment and the Multiple Functions of Educational Measurement." In *Implementing Performance Assessment: Promises, Problems, and Challenges*, ed. M. Kane and R. Mitchell, 23–38. Mahwah, NJ: Erlbaum.

Richland, L. E., O. Zur, and K. J. Holyoak. 2007. "Cognitive Supports of Analogies in the Mathematics Classroom." *Science* 316:1128–1129.

Robinson, W. S. 1950. "Ecological Correlations and the Behavior of Individuals." *American Sociological Review* 15, no. 3:351–357.

Rousseau, J. J. (1762) 1947. *The Social Contract, or Principles of Political Right.* Translated by C. Frankel. New York: Hafner.

Schacter, D. L. 1987. "Implicit Memory: History and Current Status." *Journal of Experimental Psychology: Learning, Memory, and Cognition* 13:501–518.

Schwartz, B. 2004. *The Paradox of Choice: Why More Is Less*. New York: HarperCollins.

Schwartz, D. L., and J. B. Black. 1996. "Analog Imagery in Mental Model Reasoning: Depictive Models." *Cognitive Psychology* 30:154–219.

Schwartz, D. L., and J. D. Bransford. 1998. "A Time for Telling." *Cognition and Instruction* 16:475–522.

Schwartz, D. L., J. D. Bransford, and D. Sears. 2005. "Efficiency and Innovation in Transfer." In *Transfer of Learning from a Modern Multidisciplinary Perspective*, ed. J. P. Mestre, 1–52. Greenwich, CT: Information Age Publishing.

Schwartz, D. L., C. C. Chase, D. B. Chin, M. A. Oppezzo, H. Kwong, S. Okita, G. Biswas, R. Roscoe, H. Jeong, and J. Wagster. 2009. "Interactive Metacognition: Monitoring and Regulating a Teachable Agent." In *Handbook of Metacognition in Education*, ed. D. J. Hacker, J. Dunlosky, and A. C. Graesser, 340–358. New York: Routledge.

Schwartz, D. L., C. C. Chase, M. A. Oppezzo, and D. B. Chin. 2011. "Practicing versus Inventing with Contrasting Cases: The Effects of Telling First on Learning and Transfer." *Journal of Educational Psychology* 103, no. 4:759–775.

Schwartz, D. L., and T. Martin. 2004. "Inventing to Prepare for Learning: The Hidden Efficiency of Original Student Production in Statistics Instruction." *Cognition and Instruction* 22:129–184.

Schwartz, D. L., T. Martin, and J. Chang. 2008. "Innovation and Instrumentation: Taking the Turn to Efficiency." In *Handbook of Design Research Methods in Education: Innovations in Science, Technology, Engineering, and Mathematics Learning and Teaching*, ed. A. E. Kelly, R. A. Lesh, and J. Y. Baek, 47–67. New York: Routledge.

Shaffer, D. W. 2006. *How Computer Games Help Children Learn.* New York: Macmillan.

Shavelson, R. J., G. P. Baxter, and J. Pine. 1991. "Performance Assessment in Science." *Applied Measurement in Education* 4:347–362.

Shen, C. 2002. "Revisiting the Relationship between Students' Achievement and Their Self-perceptions: A Cross-national Analysis Based on TIMSS 1999 Data. Assessment in Education: Principles." *Policy and Practice* 9, no. 2:161–184.

Shute, V. J. 2011. "Stealth Assessment in Computer-Based Games to Support Learning." In *Computer Games and Instruction,* ed. S. Tobias and J. D. Fletcher, 503–524. Charlotte, NC: Information Age Publishers.

Skinner, B. F. 1986. "Programmed Instruction Revisited." *Phi Delta Kappan* 68, no. 2:103–110.

Snow, R. 1989. "Aptitude-Treatment Interaction as a Framework for Research on Individual Differences in Learning." In *Learning and Individual Differences,* ed. P. Ackerman, R. J. Sternberg, and R. Glaser, 13–58. New York: W. H. Freeman.

Sternberg, R. J. 2006. "The Nature of Creativity." *Creativity Research Journal* 18, no. 1:87–98.

Stevens, R. H., and V. Thadani. 2007. "Quantifying Student's Scientific Problem Solving Efficiency and Effectiveness." *Technology, Instruction, Cognition, and Learning* 5:325–337.

Stroop, J. R. 1935. "Studies of Interference in Serial Verbal Reactions." *Journal of Experimental Psychology* 18, no. 6:643–662.

Tai, R. H., C. Q. Liu, A. V. Maltese, and X. Fan. 2006. "Planning Early for Careers in Science." *Science* 312:1143–1144.

Tancer, B. 2008. *Click: What Millions of People Are Doing Online and Why It Matters.* New York: Hyperion.

Taylor, J. L., K. M. Smith, A. P. van Stolk, and G. B. Spiegelman. 2010. "Using Invention to Change How Students Tackle Problems." *CBE Life Sciences Education* 8:504–512.

Tobias, S. 2009. "An Eclectic Appraisal of the Success or Failure of Constructivist Instruction." In *Constructivist Instruction: Success or Failure?* ed. S. Tobias and T. Duffy, 335–350. New York: Routledge.

Tobias, S., and T. Duffy, eds. 2009. *Constructivist Instruction: Success or Failure?* New York: Routledge.

Tversky, A., and D. Kahneman. 1974. "Judgment under Uncertainty: Heuristics and Biases." *Science* 185:1124–1131.

Vygotsky, L. S. (1934) 1987. *The Collected Works of L. S. Vygotsky*, ed. R. Rieber and A. Carton. New York: Plenum.

Wainer, H. 2010. "14 Conversations about Three Things." *Journal of Educational and Behavioral Statistics* 35, no. 1:5–25.

Watson, G., and E. Glaser. 2002. *Watson-Glaser Critical Thinking Appraisal—UK Edition: Practice Test*. London: Pearson Assessment.

Williamson, D. M., R. J. Mislevy, and I. I. Bejar. 2006. *Automated Scoring of Complex Tasks in Computer-Based Testing*. Mahwah, NJ: Lawrence Erlbaum.

Wineburg, S. 1991. "On the Reading of Historical Texts: Notes on the Breach between School and Academy." *American Educational Research Journal* 28:495–519.

Wineburg, S. 1998. "Reading Abraham Lincoln: An Expert/Expert Study in the Interpretation of Historical Texts." *Cognitive Science* 22, no. 3:319–346.

Yackel, E., and P. Cobb. 1996. "Sociomathematical Norms, Argumentation, and Autonomy in Mathematics." *Journal for Research in Mathematics Education* 27:458–477.